Media Dictatorship

Media Dictatorship

How Schools and Educators Can Defend Freedom of Speech

Cedrick Ngalande

ROWMAN & LITTLEFIELD
Lanham • Boulder • New York • London

Published by Rowman & Littlefield
An imprint of The Rowman & Littlefield Publishing Group, Inc.
4501 Forbes Boulevard, Suite 200, Lanham, Maryland 20706
www.rowman.com

86-90 Paul Street, London EC2A 4NE

British Library Cataloguing in Publication Information Available

Library of Congress Cataloging-in-Publication Data

Names: Ngalande, Cedrick, author.
Title: Media dictatorship : how schools and educators can defend freedom of speech / Cedrick Ngalande.
Description: Lanham, Maryland : Rowman & Littlefield, 2022. | Includes bibliographical references and index.
Identifiers: LCCN 2022012022 (print) | LCCN 2022012023 (ebook) |
    ISBN 9781475864328 (cloth) | ISBN 9781475864335 (paperback) |
    ISBN 9781475864342 (ebook)
Subjects: LCSH: Mass media in education—United States. | Mass media—Study and teaching—United States. | Freedom of speech—United States.
Classification: LCC LB1043 .N626 2022 (print) | LCC LB1043 (ebook) |
    DDC 371.35/8—dc23/eng/20220427
LC record available at https://lccn.loc.gov/2022012022
LC ebook record available at https://lccn.loc.gov/2022012023

This book is dedicated to Mwayi Alfred

Contents

Preface

There is a strange story, in the Bible, about the Tower of Babel. A group of people—a kingdom—believed that their God lived up in the heavens. So they decided to build a very tall tower reaching to where their God was. The people worked so hard, and the tower kept getting taller and taller, until their God became worried that his people would reach up to him. So he used his supernatural power to bring confusion among the people. The confusion was so great that the tower project crumbled. It is a very fascinating story.

Perhaps there is a "Tower of Babel syndrome" in all humankind that ensures that civilizations and kingdoms cannot grow beyond a certain point before they start destroying themselves. After all, how else can you explain why civilizations, after having built themselves to remarkable levels using particular sets of principles, eventually start gutting the very principles on which they were built?

Since its founding, the United States of America has prospered more than any nation in history. America leads the world in science and technology, military power, and economy muscle. The secret sauce to America's prosperity is the democratic principles of freedom of thought and speech. It was the dream of the founding fathers that American citizens would have freedoms to pursue knowledge and speak freely, for or against their own government.

Unfortunately, these founding principles are now under attack. The American media, whose original intention was to enrich democracy by facilitating the free flow of information, has amassed so much power for itself that it is now influencing, rather than reporting, the news. The media now controls which views are allowed in public conversations and which views are restricted. Those who go against group media think are being threatened, even to the point of losing their livelihoods. The big media tech companies, with exclusive control over public/social media fora, are increasingly censoring opinion they feel uncomfortable about. People's freedom of speech is slowly ebbing away. American democracy appears to be under threat. Is America struggling with its own "Tower of Babel syndrome"?

This book outlines how the American media uses its enormous power to control every aspect of the people's lives and government. It also discusses the devastating consequences of such control on our democracy and offers suggestions on what schools and educators can do to defend freedom of speech.

While the audience of the book is broad, it is primarily intended for educators at all levels and school administrators. The school system has always been the first line of defense for patriotism and democracy. It is important for teachers to understand the consequences of a powerful media that does not tolerate diversity of thought. The book will encourage teachers to cultivate independence of thought among students. School administrators, too, have a responsibility to ensure that school campuses are sanctuaries of freedom of thought where leaders of tomorrow are taught to be tolerant of opposing views.

To the students and the larger public, I hope to spur a robust debate about the kind of media that can help nurture our democracy.

Acknowledgments

The book would not have been possible without numerous conversations with friends and colleagues over time.

However, I would like to thank in a special way Professor Jeb Barnes of the University of Southern California, who kindly accepted to review chapter 1 of the book. His critique helped to shape the rest of the book.

Samuel Ekweghariri offered insightful analysis to the ideas in the book. Dr. Pape Sylla, my phone debate partner and very knowledgeable on a wide range of issues, was always willing to offer constructive opinions. His analysis was very helpful.

There were also many others not mentioned here. To all of them, thank you!

Introduction

Democracies are governments by the people, for the people. They respect human rights and offer their citizens a wide range of freedoms. In democracies, people are free to choose their leaders. Governments get their mandates from the people.

On the other hand, totalitarian regimes are recognized by their inability to respect human rights. Leaders are not elected by people, but rather impose themselves on the people. Citizens of these countries lose their freedoms of speech, religion, and pursuit of knowledge.

The distinction between democracies and totalitarian society has always been clear, at least until now. Democracies are characterized by free and fair elections, while totalitarian regimes always conduct sham elections.

What if a nation holds regular free and fair elections, but its citizens are denied freedoms of speech and thought, not by the government but by some unelected powerful entity within the country, should such a nation still be classified as a democracy? Even though the citizens are allowed to vote freely, the unelected powerful entity does not trust their intelligence, so they are not given full information before voting.

This book discusses the rise of media dictatorship in America, where the press has become so powerful that it is increasingly controlling every aspect of the citizens' lives. Thus, freedoms of speech and thought are being taken away. The government still holds regular free and fair elections; leaders are still changed through elections; but America can no longer be described as a democracy.

This media dictatorship is a form of dictatorship that has never been seen before in history. It is a dictatorship born of the democratic system. The free press, whose original intention was to enrich democracy, accumulates power for itself and starts controlling both the people and government. Unlike in traditional dictatorships, where either a civilian or a military junta controls everything, in the media dictatorship, it is the media establishment that is the dictator.

Regardless of the type of dictatorship, the effects of all dictatorships on a country are the same. Just as with any dictatorship, the rise of the media dictatorship in America has serious consequences to the future of nation. America was founded on the principle of freedoms of speech and thought. If those freedoms are taken away, the idea of America collapses. Science and technology—the main drivers of America's prosperity—can only thrive in a climate where scientists, philosophers, and artists are allowed the freedom to pursuit knowledge and excellence.

Chapter 1 of the book introduces the concept of media dictatorship. It does so by comparing the current situation in America to what was happening in the African country Malawi when that country was still under a dictator. The parallels between life in the days of the Malawian dictatorship and the current atmosphere in America are very alarming.

Chapter 2 explains how the media's choice tool for controlling the people is political correctness. It is the stick with which the media beats its critics into line. It covers media corruption and details how the media achieves its goal of controlling people by the way it reports the news. The media is able to shape the news without lying by simply leaving out details. Examples are given on how the media has shaped big events in the country by using this technique.

Chapter 3 exhaustively looks at the larger consequences of media dictatorships. It details how democracy, science, and freedom of thought have been damaged by the media dictatorship. Examples will be given, including the handling of the coronavirus pandemic and climate change intervention.

Chapter 4 discusses how the media influences and controls the Christian church, a demonstration of how far reaching the power of the media has become.

Chapter 5 looks at the effect of media power on universities and school campuses.

Chapter 6 goes into detail on the hypocrisy of social media platforms, and how tech giants use their platforms to push agendas by claiming to fact check on behalf of the people.

Chapter 7 summarizes the book. It also looks at the remedy for the current predicament. The chapter also offers tips on identifying misleading information, and what to do about it.

Chapter 1

The Rise of Media Dictatorship

Donald T. Sterling was the billionaire owner of the Los Angeles Clippers basketball team. On April 25, 2014, his mistress leaked a voice recording in which he had said some very unflattering things about black people.[1]

The tape sparked an unprecedented media firestorm. The media called for Sterling to be stripped of his team. He unsuccessfully apologized many times in the press. The more he appeared in the media, the more it seemed he poured gasoline on this media storm. Even Barack Obama, the president of the United States at the time, eventually commented on the tape. The president urged the National Basketball Association (NBA) commissioner to do the "right thing."[2] By April 29, Donald Sterling had been banned from the NBA and lost the team he had owned. The mighty American media had once again demonstrated its immense power.

The American press is very powerful. It can influence many decisions and actions in society, it can influence prices and quantities, and it also has the potential to manipulate the democratic process.[3]

Donald Sterling was not the first person to be punished by the media. The list of victims includes politicians, talk show hosts, business executives, and people from all walks of life. Casual observers will quickly point to the crassness of Sterling's remarks and justify the intense media storm and the eventual loss of ownership his basketball team.

The truth is that the media chooses whom to penalize based on its special interests. In other words, the media exercises power and control over people by choosing to highlight only those stories that perpetuate its power, and suppresses or ignores stories that are not in its interest. The motivation of the media in controlling how stories are disseminated is not unlike that of a totalitarian ruler of a third world country, for the goal of both is to control people.

The media has become so powerful that it now influences all aspects of life from politics to science, from religion to culture. In politics, the media has become the real kingmaker of presidential elections.

3

For a long time, the media in America literary picked presidents. The media would tell the public whom to vote for and whom to shun. The media would tell the people not to vote for a "Howard Dean" because he screamed[4] or a "Rick Perry" because he forgot his lines in a presidential debate.[5]

Like many things in America, the American press is largely divided into two groups—the liberal and conservative media. Liberal media comprises networks and newspapers like MSNBC, CNN, Daily Kos, Huffington Post, and so on, while the conservative media comprises Fox News, the *New York Post*, the *Washington Times*, OAN, and so on.

These two media groups report and analyze news differently based on the ideology. It is common knowledge that conservatives and liberals tend to see issues differently. According to the *Stanford Encyclopedia of Philosophy*, many philosophical commentators define conservatism as a "standpoint that is sceptical of abstract reasoning in politics, and that appeals instead to living tradition, allowing for the possibility of limited political reform."[6]

Conservative prescriptions are based on experience. In conservatism, the universe is treated as having fundamental principles, much like science. The assumption is that something will work everywhere in a particular way because it worked that same way in the past—just as in science, where water was H_2O yesterday and will be H_2O tomorrow regardless of whether one is in Johannesburg, South Africa, or Los Angeles, California.

John Kekes defines conservativism as a political morality with a fundamental aim of conserving political arrangements that have shown themselves to be conducive to good lives thus understood.[7]

Conservatists, Kekes writes,

> turn to their history not only for possibilities that make lives good, but also for limits that good lives must observe. They reflect on their history in order to understand what deserves their allegiance and what is inimical to having a good society. To conserve good political arrangements and to avoid bad ones often requires the adaptation of traditional arrangements to changing circumstances. Conservatism, therefore, does not involve strict adherence to a rigid pattern, but a flexible rearrangement of the relative importance of the elements that constitute such complex wholes as political arrangements are.[8]

According to the *Encyclopedia Britannica*, liberalism is a "political doctrine that takes protecting and enhancing the freedom of the individual to be the central problem of politics. Liberals typically believe that government is necessary to protect individuals from being harmed by others, but they also recognize that government itself can pose a threat to liberty."[9]

American society is defined by conservatism and liberalism in a big way. There are the conservative and liberal political parties, churches, judges, think tanks, and so on. It should, therefore, not be surprising that the media too is divided into conservative and liberal media.

Both the liberal and conservative media try to put a spin on their reporting to advance their ideology. In the process, journalists become activists striving to prove a point or promote an agenda, rather than reporting the news. A single event can be reported very differently by the two media groups.

Take for instance, the reporting on Dr. Anthony Fauci's testimony before the US Senate Health Education Labor and Pensions Committee on Tuesday July 20, 2021. Dr. Fauci heads the US National Institute of Allergy and Infectious Diseases (NIAID) and is also chief medical advisor to President Biden's COVID response team. He was called before the senate to give an update on federal response to the COVID pandemic.[10]

During the hearing, Kentucky senator Rand Paul asked Dr. Fauci whether NIH ever funded gain-of-function research at the Wuhan Institute of Virology. The term *gain-of-function research* describes a type of research that modifies a biological agent so that new or enhanced activity is conferred to that agent.[11]

What followed was a fascinating and passionate exchange between Senator Paul and Dr. Fauci. The subject is highly technical, and it became quickly evident that such a debate could not be resolved in just six minutes. It would certainly take experts a significant amount of time to settle it.

It is interesting to see how the media reported this Paul-Fauci exchange. The liberal media was more interested in portraying Dr. Fauci as very reasonable and Senator Paul as ignorant. Liberal news networks only emphasized the part where Dr. Fauci said, "Senator Paul, you don't know what you are talking about."[12]

For the liberal media, it was important that Dr. Fauci be seen as winning this debate. Ever since the 2020 coronavirus pandemic began, the media had sought to tie the problem to former president Donald Trump, whom they detested. Dr. Fauci became the Trump counterpoint they relied upon. In the liberal world, Dr. Fauci's words were watched carefully, protected, defended, and cherished as gospel truth. In fact, during the 2020 US vice presidential debate, candidate Kamala Harris went so far as to suggest that she would not take any vaccine developed under President Trump unless Dr. Fauci said told her to do so.[13]

Mary Katherine Ham perfectly summed up the liberal media's reporting on Dr. Fauci when, appearing on CNN, she accused the liberal media of "fangirling" for Fauci.[14]

On the other hand, the conservative media concentrated more on what they perceived to be Dr. Fauci's faults. In the conservative circles, Dr. Fauci was seen as more political and opportunistic than scientific.

The stark difference in the ways the two media groups report same events was also seen in the way Black Lives Matter (BLM) and the January 6

Capital riots were reported. In the summer of 2020, violent riots broke out across the United States following the killing of George Floyd, a black man, by the police. BLM demonstrations erupted across the country with quite a few turning into violent protests,[15] resulting in destruction of property[16] and loss of life.[17]

While the conservative media mostly described the BLM riots as barbaric and irresponsible, the liberal media was at pains to portray the riots as peaceful civil rights demonstrations.[18] In a now famous video clip, an MSNBC reporter stands in front of a burning and looted store and claims that "the demonstrations have all been peaceful."[19]

The same liberal media, meanwhile, changed its tune when it came to reporting the so-called January 6 Capitol Hill demonstrators. On January 6, 2021, supporters of former president Trump gathered in Washington, DC, to attend a rally by President Trump, who had been claiming that the recent presidential election had been rigged against him. After listening to the president, the demonstrators went to the capital to demand that Congress stop certifying the declared winner, Joe Biden, as president. The demonstration broke into a riot that resulted in people overrunning the Capitol.

The liberal media described these mostly unarmed rural demonstrators, first, as coup plotters[20] and then as dangerous insurrectionists.[21] When the FBI eventually found no evidence of coordinated efforts to overthrow government,[22] the liberal media abruptly dropped the story without highlighting the FBI finding. A quick search through news archives will show that most of the media silently edited titles of their old news reports to remove incendiary terms such as "coup" or "insurrection."

The difference in reporting between conservative and liberal media is also seen in the way the story concerning Fox News host Tucker Carlson and the National Security Agency (NSA) was covered. On June 28, 2021, Tucker Carlson informed his audience that he had learned through a whistleblower that the NSA was spying on him.

Immediately, the liberal media cast doubt on the story.[23]

On July 24, 2021, liberal and conservative media groups gave two entirely different updates on the story. CNN's headline said, "NSA Review Finds No Evidence Supporting Tucker Carlson's Claims NSA Was Spying on Him, Sources Say,"[24] whereas the *New York Post*'s heading for the same story was, "Tucker Carlson's 'Unmasking' Claim Confirmed by NSA Investigators: Report."[25]

Clearly, liberal and conservative media report events so differently that those who watch liberal media exclusively could have a vastly different understanding of events from those who watch only conservative media. While diversity in media philosophy is a good thing, in the American context, there is a huge imbalance between the gigantic liberal media and the small conservative media. The imbalance is so great that, more generally, the American media can be described as having a liberal bias and slanted far to the left of its audience.[26]

True, conservatives have a strong presence on the radio. However, in the grand scheme of things, radio has little influence when one considers the whole media realm. In fact, a study by Andrea Prat of Columbia university has shown that, despite the presence of radio and social media, the four most powerful media organizations in the United States are still television providers.[27]

A 2004 study by Tim Groseclose and Jeffrey Milyo found a strong liberal bias in the media.[28] While most studies and discussions about media bias are subjective, this study used a scientific and quantifiable method to measure media bias.

Groseclose and Milyo's method determined the bias of a news outlet by observing the number of times the outlet cited certain think tanks and policy groups. They then compared this data with the number of times US congressmen cited the same think tanks and policy groups in their speeches on the floors of the Senate or House.

If the pattern of citation matched, then that particular network was considered to have the same political ideology as the congressman. Thus, for example, the *New York Times* would be more likely to cite the same think tanks and policy groups as former Massachusetts senator Ted Kennedy.

Perhaps it should not be surprising that the media has a strong liberal bias. Surveys have shown that a large fraction of journalists are liberal.[29] A study by Elaine Povich found that in the 1992 US presidential elections, 7 percent of Washington correspondents voted for the Republican presidential candidate (George H. W. Bush) and 89 percent voted for the Democratic presidential candidate (Bill Clinton).[30]

Even though Bush lost that election, the 7 percent he got from the Washington correspondents is far less than the 37 percent of the vote the American public gave him.

According to a *New York Times* news article of August 1, 2004,[31] only 8 percent of the Washington correspondents believed that Republican candidate George W. Bush would be a better president than Democrat John Kerry. In contrast, 51 percent of Americans thought Bush would make a better president. This is important because Washington, DC, is the de facto headquarters of the American media.

Using data from the Center for Responsive Politics, *New York Times* op-ed columnists David Brooks observed that "among journalists, there were 93 Kerry donors for every one Bush donor."[32]

In their study of media bias, Groseclose and Milyo found that of the twenty prominent news outlets, eighteen were either left of center or entirely on the left.[33] Only Fox News and the *Washington Times* were conservative; CNN *NewsNight* with Aaron Brown, the *PBS NewsHour* with Jim Lehrer, and ABC's *Good Morning America* were found to be the most balanced.

Of course, the CNN referred to in the Groseclose and Milyo study was starkly different from the new CNN. At the time, CNN was considered centrist and factual.[34] Now CNN has moved to the left and become more opinionated.

In the article "The New CNN Is More Opinionated and Emotional. Can It Still Be 'The Most Trusted Name in News'?" Jeremy Barr describes the new CNN as a place "where journalists and anchors, traditionally restricted by industry-wide standards of impartiality, have been given the green light under network President Jeff Zucker to say what they actually want to say—even if it strikes some as opinionated."[35]

Barr observes that the new CNN is a far cry from the old CNN, a network that had built its reputation on studiously neutral impartiality. The new CNN entertains emotional rawness that would have certainly been regarded as bias under the old CNN standards.[36]

Barr gives examples of the new CNN's lack of neutrality such as when Jake Tapper said, after the Biden election, "For tens of millions of our fellow Americans, their long, national nightmare is over." Or, when Don Lemon confessed on air, during the Derek Chauvin trial, that he was anxious to see what the value of a black life is. And, then went on to proclaim, "Justice has been served!" after Derek Chauvin's conviction.[37]

And, of course, there was Jim Acosta's public personal animosity against former president Trump that could not be justified under any journalistic standards.

It is interesting to note that Fox News, generally considered a conservative boogeyman by the liberal media, is not as conservative as most liberal outlets are liberal. While featuring only conservative opinion-show hosts in the evening, Fox News has an array of fairly diverse hosts during the day.

Fox News host Neil Cavuto and former host Chris Wallace,[38] can be described as having on-air views that are at the center or left of center. There are no corresponding anchors on CNN or MSNBC who are anything other than left or left of center. CNN, MSNBC, and the entire mainstream media are very homogeneous in opinion and philosophy.

Media bias is also perceived on social platforms. A 2020 PEW study found that 69 percent of Republicans/Republican-leaners and 25 percent of Democrats /Democratic-leaners believe that technology companies generally support the views of liberals over conservatives. Nearly 90 percent of Republicans believe that social media sites censor political viewpoints.[39]

Since the media has become powerful and very partisan, this imbalance of coverage results in a power imbalance, so much that American independents and conservatives feel like they are living under liberal dictatorship.

Since the American media is heavily skewed toward the left, henceforth in this book, "media" will be used to mean "liberal, mainstream, or leftist media."

The media in America tend to single out, scrutinize, harass, and often punish conservatives for their views. Take for instance the coverage of former president Donald Trump. From the moment he announced his run for the president in 2015 right to the end of his presidency and even beyond, some twenty-four-hour cable networks filled all their time and programming with anti-Trump material. He was constantly being referred to as a "racist," the worst label for any American in the twenty-first century.

Whenever people in the media were asked why they constantly referred to Trump as a racist, the answers were often less than convincing. Vox compiled what it called Donald Trump's long history of racism from the 1970s to the 2000s.[40] Chief among these was the allegation that in 1973 a federal lawsuit was brought against Trump and his company for alleged racial discrimination at Trump housing developments in New York.

It is interesting to note that the media did not label Joe Biden a racist for his many wrong positions and statements on race. Although he now downplays his involvement, Biden was a central figure in the crime bill that the *New York Times* describes as "groundwork for the mass incarceration that has devastated America's black communities."[41]

In his own words on the Senate floor, Biden declared that when it came to taking criminals off the street "it does not matter whether or not they were deprived as a youth; it does not matter whether or not they had no background that enabled them to become socialized into the fabric of the society. It doesn't matter whether or not they are the victims of the society. The end result is that they are about to knock my mother with a lead pipe on the head, shoot my sister, beat up my wife, take on my sons. So, I don't want to ask what made them do this. They must be taken off the street!"[42]

Over his political career, Mr. Biden has at times aligned himself with segregationists, and even sometimes used incendiary language such as "Predators on our streets," "Lock the S.O.B.s up," "George H. W. Bush not doing enough to put 'violent thugs' in prison."[43]

Incidentally, even two years after Trump was sued for alleged housing discrimination, Joe Biden was still fighting student busing.[44] Yet the media, in spite of this record, does not label Joe Biden as racist.

The other major allegation listed by Vox was that Trump had pushed the notion that former US president Barack Obama was born in Kenya. The relationship between pushing this erroneous notion that Obama was born in

Kenya and racism is very unclear. Vox claimed that research has shown a correlation between the two. Vox did not cite the research.

Some claimed that such an erroneous claim was racist because it was meant to make Obama an illegitimate president. Here again is another weak argument. Everybody knew that Mr. Obama's mother was a white American citizen. Whether she gave birth while in Kenya, India, or Canada, her son—Obama—would still be a natural born citizen and therefore eligible for the presidency.

There is no doubt that Barack Obama was born in the United States. However, accusing those who erroneously claim that Obama was born in Kenya of racism, is in itself racist. If the claim was that either Obama or Biden was born in Ireland, those same people would not have thought that such a claim was racist. Clearly, their opinion of Kenya is so low that they think such a country should not be associated in any way with an American president.

Some in the media would also point to Trump's many other statements as being insensitive and therefore a sign that he is a racist.[45] The same media, however, largely overlooked disgustingly horrible racist comments by Harry Reid, former senator from Nevada.

Senator Reid holds the distinction for saying one of the most racially incendiary statements by any politician ever. He was the Democratic Senate majority leader from 2007 to 2015. When Barack Obama first announced his candidacy for president, Harry Reid observed that Obama was likely to win the presidency as the first black man to do so because he was "a light-skinned black man with no Negro dialect, unless he wanted to have one."[46]

The fundamental pillar of racism is skin color. The superiority of white skin color over black or darker skin color has been at the core of racism throughout Western history. Even as recently as the eighteenth century, a debate was still going on as to whether black skin is normal. In the 1790s some influential people of the time, like Benjamin Rush, were advancing theories that black skin was a defect possibly because of diseases like leprosy.[47]

This philosophy, though hidden today, still manifests itself in the beauty and TV industries where perfection is still based on Caucasian features. Thus, by pointing to Obama's light skin color as a qualification a black person needs for the presidency, Harry Reid was appealing to the worst angels of racism. In doing so, he insulted millions of capable dark-skinned black people, who in some cases are held back by their skin color.

You would think that the media, which claims to use its power for the good of society, would take such a person to task and maybe even call for his resignation. That is not what happened. The media mentioned the incident only briefly, and when Harry Reid apologized to Obama, the media completely dropped the story.

Harry Reid continued to be the majority leader in the Senate. In fact, it is very ironic that when Harry apologized, he apologized to Obama, not to the millions of dark-skinned black people he actually offended with such a remark.[48]

This is an example of the media using its power, not for public good, but to achieve its goals. They attacked conservative Donald Trump for comments they implied were racist but then largely gave a pass to liberal Harry Reid's direct racist statement.

The same media double standard is also seen in the way the media deals with conservative and liberal personalities. For example, it appears the media does not tolerate racial slurs or insensitive remarks except when the intended target is a conservative. There are numerous times when conservatives like Senator Tim Scott,[49] Dr. Ben Carlson.[50] Larry Elder,[51] and Justice Clarence Thomas[52] have been described in the press as Uncle Toms by media personalities with no consequences to the speaker.

As was the case of Donald Sterling, the media uses its immerse power to punish people who say things that the media believes should not be said. In short, the media protects its power over the people by threatening to take the livelihood of those who insist on exercising their freedom of speech contrary to the media's view of the world. The media believes that there is only one view of the world, and those who do not subscribe to it must be destroyed or taken out of the public debate, that is, if one still exists at all.

The tendency to victimize people for their beliefs or opinion, though relatively new within the United States, has always been present outside America. Take the example of Malawi, a country in southeastern Africa.

Malawi, formerly Nyasaland, was a British colony until it became independent in 1964. The liberation movement against the British colonial government was led by Dr. Hastings Kamuzu Banda. Before coming back to Malawi, Banda had spent many years in America and Britain where he was trained and had a successful career as a medical doctor.

As the first president of Malawi and the first black man to publicly challenge white rulers in that country, Banda became very popular and even revered. Banda took advantage of his popularity and consolidated his power by banning freedom of speech and rival political parties. He created one of the most infamous repressive dictatorships in Africa.[53] Opposition of any kind was not allowed.[54]

It is quite interesting to see the similarities between the old dictatorship Malawi and the current American media-led censorship. The parallels are alarming. Just like the people of America who cannot fully express themselves for fear of being humiliated by the press and losing their jobs, the people of Malawi in those days of dictatorship could not express themselves for fear of the dictator.

In fact, there are many more similarities between the Malawi dictatorship and the current climate in America.

In the Malawi dictatorship, branding was used as a form of propaganda to incite the general public against those who disagreed with the authorities. The media would use unnecessarily scary terms to accomplish its task. For instance, anybody who had a different opinion or disagreement with the Malawi dictator would be branded as a dangerous "dissident" or a "rebel" that needed to be dealt with to save the country. Does this sound familiar?

In the America of today, the January 6, 2021, rioters who stormed the US Capitol are being described in heavy terms such as "insurrectionists" or "coup plotters."[55] In fact, the rioters' claim that the 2020 election was rigged has been branded "The Big Lie."

Claims of fraud in elections are not new in America or elsewhere. In their landmark paper "Classifying Political Regimes," Alverez et al. observed that, in fact, baseless allegations of fraud are frequent in elections, and that "screaming 'fraud' is just a standard repertoire of democratic competition."[56]

It should be pointed out that the same media that was angry about the so-called Big Lie in 2021 looked the other way when Hillary Clinton claimed that the 2016 election was stolen from her.[57] In fact, her supporters had staged violent riots in Washington, DC, during Donald Trump's inauguration.[58]

Another similarity between the old Malawi and the current America is seen in the prevalence of conspiracy theories. The Malawian press was so biased in their reporting that nobody believed them. As such conspiracy theories abounded, citizens appeared to believe the word of a neighbor more than what they heard in the media. Just like it was in the old Malawi, so it is in America today. The America of today is also full of conspiracy theories. The media, because of its obvious bias and desire to amass power for itself, has lost its credibility in the eyes of a large section of American citizens.[59]

According to a 2020 Gallup/Knight Foundation survey, three in four people believed that media company owners influence news coverage, and more than half of Americans believed that reporters misrepresent the facts.[60]

The Reuters Institute for the Study of Journalism found that in 2021, the United States ranked last in media trust—at 29 percent—among 92,000 news consumers surveyed in 46 countries. Poland, the Philippines, and Peru did better than the United States in this study.[61]

As trust erodes in the media, citizens tend to be vulnerable to conspiracy theories. Another media similarity between Malawi and the United States is the manner in which agendas are pushed in the news. Malawian media anchors used large panels of "experts" who all said the same thing. The size of the panels was intended to assure the people that there was only one side to the story, and everybody else who matters agrees with it. Just like in Malawi then, so in America today.

On different news networks in America today, it is not uncommon to see large panels on political talk shows. These panelists usually say the same thing, as if there is no other side of the story. Numerous times, these experts have unanimously predicted a huge victory for a media-supported candidate, only to find out that the results were different.

In American TV climate change debates, almost no disagreement is allowed because it is deemed dangerous. Experts who question some aspect of the media-agreed theory either lose their jobs or are permanently excommunicated from the media. All "experts" who speaks on climate issues on TV are expected to toe the same line. This is almost reminiscent of Galileo, who was imprisoned in 1633 by the dictatorship of his day, for arguing that the Earth revolves around the sun, and not vice versa as claimed by scientists and religious leaders of the time.

In the dictatorship of Malawi, "experts" who supported the dictator and toed the media were described as "world class" or legendary in their fields. It was the press, not the experts' peers, that decided who the eminent people of different fields of study were. Usually, such choices were based on those experts' tacit support of government.

As it was in Malawi, so it is in America today. During the 2020–2022 coronavirus pandemic, the US media crowned certain individuals as "eminent scientists." This is strange because the quality of a scientist is determined not by the media but by his peers. The media, being mostly composed of non-scientists, is in no position to know who a good scientist is. Not surprisingly, therefore, most of those that have been coronated as "eminent scientists" were those whose views appeared favorable to popular political viewpoints in the media.

One consequence of this media control of the coronavirus discussion is that many obvious questions were not asked. For instance, what was the scientific rationale for demanding that people wear masks outdoors? What was the scientific basis for the idea that to protect each other from the spread of the disease, people must stand at least six feet from each other? Why is it that no scientist asked these questions on TV?

Prominent Malawian diplomatic and politician Sam Mpasu[62] talked of the lack of empathy the dictatorship had on dissenting voices in Malawi during Dr Banda's reign. Those who voiced open disagreement or dissent had their careers destroyed and their businesses and property confiscated, leaving their families in need.[63]

Although not as brutal, it is not uncommon to similarly see people in modern America losing their livelihoods for comments they made in the media. TV commentors, corporate America bosses, and government officials have lost their jobs for saying politically incorrect things that are not necessarily incorrect.

Another similarity between modern America and Dr. Banda's Malawi is the use of political correctness as a tool for controlling the people. For instance, Banda used political correctness to endear himself to women citizens. He basically rewrote the history of Malawi, giving women an exaggerated role in the liberation movement. Although the government was run mostly by men, Banda created a perception that it is the women who are powerful and run the affairs of the country.

Just like Dr. Banda, the American media uses a lot of political correctness to consolidate its own power. The role of political correctness in the American media's quest for power will be discussed in detail in the next chapter.

In Dr. Banda's Malawi, religious bodies were expected to toe a certain line if they wanted to continue operating freely in the country. Jehovah's Witnesses were banned and persecuted because they refused to pay taxes. Dr. Banda had ordered that every male over the age of eighteen should pay a certain amount of tax regardless of whether they were employed or not. In a country where the vast majority of people were just peasant farmers, such a tax burden brought enormous hardship on the people.

When Jehovah's Witnesses protested, citing their beliefs, Dr. Banda ordered them banned. Dr. Banda's paramilitary wing went door to door looking for the Jehovah's Witness faithful, especially at night.

It is tempting to consider Malawi of those days as primitive. Unfortunately, America of today is not too far from that. Religious denominations in America today are not completely free to say what they believe especially when such beliefs are politically incorrect. They are afraid of harassment and demonization by the press, and even loss of tax-exempt status.

In a true democratic society, people should be able to practice their religion freely without fear of being attacked, harassed, threatened, or demonized. One does not have to agree with those politically incorrect church beliefs.

If Dr. Banda's Malawi dictatorship treated its citizens not very differently from the way American citizens are treated by their own unelected media, why is America called a democracy and not a media-run dictatorship? Is America a dictatorship?

To date, only five types of dictatorships have been known in history. These are military dictatorships, personalist dictatorships, single-party dictatorships, monarchic dictatorships and hybrid dictatorships.[64]

Military dictatorships are ruled by a military junta. To qualify as a military dictatorship, all top elite or leadership of the country, not just the leader of the regime, must be members of the military.[65] In military dictatorships, the junta makes all decisions.

Examples of military dictatorships are: Algeria (1992–present), Argentina (1943–1946; 1955–1958; 1966–1973; 1976–1983), Brazil (1964–1985), Guatemala (1970–1985), Honduras (1972–1981), Nigeria (1966–1979;

1983–1993), Peru (1968–1980), South Korea (1961–1987), Turkey (1980–1983), and Uruguay (1973–1984).[66]

Single-party dictatorships are dictatorships in which one political party wields party in the country. Other parties may exist and may even compete for elections and hold legislative seats. But the ultimate power lies within that single party.

Single-party dictatorships are usually controlled by the politburo—the central executive committee of the ruling party.

Bolivia was a single-party dictatorship from 1952 to 1964 with the Revolutionary Nationalist Movement (MNR) as the ruling party. Other examples of single-party dictatorship are: Botswana (1966–present, Botswana Democratic Party [BDP]), China (1949–present, Chinese Communist Party [CCP]), East Germany (1945–1990, Socialist Unity Party of Germany [SUPG]), Kenya (1963–2002, Kenya National African Union [KANU]), Laos (1975–present, Laos People's Revolutionary Party [LPRP]), Malaysia (1957–present, Barisan Nasional [BN]), Mexico (1917–2000, Institutional Revolutionary Party [PR]), Singapore (1965–present, People's Action Party [PAP]) and the Soviet Union (1917–1991, Communist Party [CP]).[67]

In personalist dictatorships, one person controls everything. Everything in the country is done in his name. His picture is everywhere and, in most cases, he enjoys a cultish respect. Dr. Banda of Malawi was that kind of dictator. He was almost a semi-god. It was hard to envision that he would one day die. Most people born under his rule could not have imagined any other person being called the president of Malawi.

Other examples of personalist dictatorships are: Central African Republic (1966–1979, Jean-Bedel Bokassa), Dominican Republic (1930–1961, Rafael Trujillo), Haiti (1957–1986, Francois and Jean-Claude Duvalier), Iraq (1979–2003, Saddam Hussein), Somalia (1969–1990, Siad Barre), Spain (1939–1979, Francisco Franco), Uganda (1966–1979, Milton Obote and Idi Amin), Yemen (1978–present, Ali Abdullar Salih) and Zaire (1965–1997, Joseph Mobutu).[68]

Monarchic dictatorships are dictatorships where a monarch exercises real political power, and top government leadership/elite comprises the royal family.

Some examples of monarchic dictatorships are: Afghanistan (1929–1973), Cambodia (1953–1970), Ethiopia (1850s–1974), Iran (1925–1979), Iraq (1932–1958), Jordan (1946–present), Libya (1951–1968), Oman (1940s–present), Saudi Arabia (1927–present), Eswatini (1968–present), United Arab Emirates (1971–present).[69]

Hybrid dictatorships are dictatorships that are a combination of two or more types of dictatorships, such as personalist/singe party dictatorships, personalist/military dictatorships, and so on.

If America is a dictatorship, what kind of dictatorship is it?

Alvarez et al. defined a democracy as a country where government offices are filled with contest elections. The nation's chief executive and legislature must be elected, and there must be more than one party.

Yet not all countries meeting this criterion are classified as democracies, as the case of Botswana shows.

A lot of people in southern Africa are usually shocked when they to see Botswana classified as a dictatorship. Botswana has always held free and fair elections, has opposition parties, and has had presidents step down after their terms of office. On the face of it, Botswana would seem to fit the definition of a democracy.

As Alvarez et al. pointed out, Botswana cannot be described as a democracy because, despite being a multiparty system with free and fair elections, only one party has won elections since 1966. It is not known whether that one party will concede power when they lose an election. Thus, the classification should err on the side of Botswana being a dictatorship. This means that a nation can have almost all of the regular characteristics of a democracy and still not be a full democracy.

To most people, it is absurd to ask whether the America of 2021 is still a democracy. The question does not look so stupid when one starts analyzing it. Bollen lists "fairness of elections" as one of the measures of popular sovereignty.[70] Thus, of one the major characteristics of a democracy is that the country's political leaders are elected in regularly held fair elections. The question now becomes whether elections, regularly held in America, qualify to be called free elections.

By America's own definition of a free and fair election, America does not hold free and fair elections. Of course, this discussion is not about stuffing of ballot boxes or fraud as was alleged in the 2020 presidential elections. To date, no evidence has been shown to prove that the 2020 presidential elections in America were stolen through the stuffing of ballot boxes or fraud.

The position of the US government is that a country cannot be truly democratic until its citizens have the opportunity to choose their representatives through free and fair elections. The American government believes that ten elements are essential to fair elections and political processes.[71]

These elements are:[72] 1) impartial electoral frameworks, 2) credible electoral administration, 3) effective oversight of electoral processes, 4) informed and active citizens, 5) representative and competitive multiparty systems, 6) effective governance by elected leaders and bodies, 7) inclusion of women and disadvantaged groups, 8) effective transfer of political power, 9) consensus-building for democratic reform, and 10) sustainable local engagement.

Notice that the fourth element names "informed and active citizenry" as a perquisite to a free and fair election. The only way citizens can be reasonably informed is when the press is free and balanced. The coverage of presidential elections in America, certainly the 2020 elections, was far from fair and balanced. Thus, it is safe to conclude that, judging by America's own yardstick for free elections, America's elections do not pass muster because of element number 4.

In 2020, press coverage of the US presidential elections was so one-sided and so pro candidate Joe Biden that he spent very little time campaigning and faced very little scrutiny. In that sense, the American people could not be said to have been well informed. Questions that would normally feature highly in presidential election analysis were this time brushed aside when they involved candidate Joe Biden's health and/or family business.[73]

Even social media did not provide a free platform. The social media giant Twitter prevented free discussion of allegations of corruption by Joe Biden's son. The *New York Post* was banned on Twitter for carrying a story about the alleged corruption.[74]

In the past, America has rejected election results in Zimbabwe[75] and other closed countries simply because, among other things, the press coverage was not balanced. The slanted coverage in 2020 elections was not unlike election coverage in dictatorships or totalitarian countries. The only difference was that in America, the slanted coverage was toward the challenger, not the incumbent.

So, if America is not a full democracy, which category of dictatorship would it lean toward? America does not fit any of the categories of dictatorships defined by experts thus far. Yet it cannot be a full democracy with a media slanted so much in one direction. The American electorate is not informed enough for elections in America to be fully free and fair.

While all the other dictatorships control people through the media, the uniqueness of the American dictatorship would be that the media itself has evolved into the dictator. The American dictatorship could, therefore, be described as "media dictatorship."

While it is an outrageous exaggeration to say that America of 2021 is exactly at the level of the Malawi dictatorship, it is also naïve to dismiss the ever-growing signs of a clear and present dictatorship. Of course, even as a form of dictatorship, America would be more organized and methodical than the Malawi dictatorship. This is because the Malawian dictatorship, as a personalist dictatorship, was vulnerable to eccentric policies that, according to Ezrow and Frantz, usually characterize personalist dictatorships.[76]

Some will say that the American media is simply looking out for the people, and that its intentions are pure. Unfortunately, this also happens to be the same argument dictators make for their repressive policies. Dictators believe that they are looking out for the good of their countries; they think they are smarter than the people they lead; they don't trust the people to make their own decisions.

In fact, it is not unusual for oppressive powers to think that their subjects support their way of running the society. Dr. Banda of Malawi once said, "I am a dictator of the people. I dictate by permission, by consent . . . should people as a whole tire of me and my party, then they will remove and replace us."[77] The irony is that no rival parties or dissenting voices were allowed in Malawi at the time.

Former Zimbabwean dictator, Robert Mugabe, claimed that Zimbabweans still need him, "If people say you are a dictator . . . they are saying this merely to tarnish you and diminish and demean your status. My people still need me and when people still need you to lead them, it's not time, sir, doesn't matter how old you are, to say goodbye."[78]

As for apartheid, former South African president Pieter Willem Botha reportedly believed that "most blacks are happy, except those who have had other ideas pushed into their ears."[79]

In America today, the media seems to have assumed the role of a dictator. Unlike traditional dictatorships, where an individual, family, or military controls a country, in America it is the media that has amassed tremendous, unchecked power. The media is so powerful that it controls speech, debates, politics, and policies. Those who argue for positions contrary to what the media advocates are demeaned and vilified.

This is dangerous because our civilization—the modern civilization—is based on freedom of thought and pursuit of knowledge. Those principles are what has given us democracy and all the technological advances. The future of our civilization cannot be secure if we start gutting the very principles on which it was founded.

This book outlines how the American media uses its enormous power to control every aspect of the people's lives and government. It also discusses the devastating consequences of such control on our democracy and offers suggestions on what schools and educators can do to defend freedom of speech.

While the audience of the book is wide, it is primarily intended for educators, at all levels, and school administrators. The school system has always been the first line of defense for patriotism and democracy. It is important for teachers to understand the consequences of a powerful media that does not tolerate diversity of thought. The book will encourage teachers to cultivate independence of thought among students. School administrators, too, have a responsibility to ensure that school campuses are sanctuaries of freedom of thought where leaders of tomorrow are taught to be tolerant of opposing views.

NOTES

1. Yglesias, Matthew. "Donald Sterling's racist outburst," Vox, May 13, 2015. https://www.vox.com/2014/4/29/18077046/donald-sterling

2. Carroll, Rory. "Obama leads backlash against LA Clippers owner's alleged racist remarks," *The Guardian*, April 27, 2014. https://www.theguardian.com/world/2014/apr/27/david-sterling-clippers-racist-recording-obama-backlash

3. Prat, Andrea. "Media power," *Journal of Political Economy* 126, no. 4 (July 2018): 1747–83.

4. Walsh, Kenneth, T. "The battle cry that backfired on Howard 'The Scream' Dean," *US News & World Report*, January 17, 2008. https://www.usnews.com/news/articles/2008/01/17/the-battle-cry-that-backfired

5. Gardner, Amy, and Rucker, Phillip. "Rick Perry stumbles badly in Republican presidential debate," *The Guardian*, April 27, 2014. https://www.washingtonpost.com/politics/republican-presidential-candidates-focus-on-economy/2011/11/09/gIQA5Lsp6M_story.html

6. Hamilton, Andy, "Conservatism," *The Stanford Encyclopedia of Philosophy* (Spring 2020), Edward N. Zalta (ed.). https://plato.stanford.edu/archives/spr2020/entries/conservatism/

7. Kekes, John. "What is conservatism?" *Philosophy* 72, no. 281 (1997): 351–74. http://www.jstor.org/stable/3751738

8. Ibid.

9. Girvetz, H. K., Ball, Terence, Minogue, Kenneth, and Dagger, Richard. "Liberalism" *Encyclopedia Britannica*, February 5, 2020. https://www.britannica.com/topic/liberalism

10. C-SPAN Video. "Senate hearing on COVID-19 response," C-SPAN, July 20, 2021. https://www.c-span.org/video/?513400-1/senate-hearing-covid-19-response

11. "Gain-of-function research involving potential pandemic pathogens," National Institute of Health, July 20, 2021. https://www.nih.gov/news-events/gain-function-research-involving-potential-pandemic-pathogens

12. Janfaza, Rachel. "Fauci and Rand Paul have terse exchange: 'You do not know what you are talking about,'" CNN, July 20, 2021. https://www.cnn.com/2021/07/20/politics/anthony-fauci-rand-paul-debate/index.html

13. Hernandez, Salvador. "Kamala Harris said she wouldn't take a COVID vaccine only recommended by Trump," Buzzfeed, October 7, 2020. https://www.buzzfeednews.com/article/salvadorhernandez/kamala-harris-covid-vaccine-vp-debate

14. Marsh, Kristine. "FIREWORKS! on CNN, Mary Katharine Ham shames media 'fangirling' for Fauci," Newsbusters, July 21, 2021. https://newsbusters.org/blogs/nb/kristine-marsh/2021/07/21/fireworks-cnn-mary-katharine-ham-shames-media-fangirling-fauci

15. Casiano, Louis. "Police chief association releases number of officers injured during violent riots," Fox News, December 1, 2020. https://www.foxnews.com/us/police-chief-officers-injured-riots

16. Manskar, Noah. "Riots following George Floyd's death may cost insurance companies up to $2B," *New York Post*, September 16, 2020. https://nypost.com/2020/09/16/riots-following-george-floyds-death-could-cost-up-to-2b/

17. Cullinane, Susannah. "Retired St. Louis Police captain killed after responding to a pawnshop alarm during looting," CNN, August 27, 2020. https://www.cnn.com/2020/06/03/us/david-dorn-st-louis-police-shot-trnd/index.html

18. Murray, Paul. "BLM riots caused over $1 billion of damage, 'yet media says they're mostly peaceful,'" Sky News Australia, September 17, 2020. https://www.youtube.com/watch?v=TcOJh6hzzj8

19. Wulfsohn, Joseph. "MSNBC's Ali Velshi says situation not 'generally speaking unruly' while standing outside burning building," Fox News, May 29, 2020. https://www.foxnews.com/media/msnbc-anchor-says-minneapolis-carnage-is-mostly-a-protest-as-building-burns-behind-him

20. Wagner, Meg, et al. "Jake Tapper: 'We're watching an attempt at sedition,'" CNN, January 6, 2021, 3:33 PM EST. https://www.cnn.com/politics/live-news/congress-electoral-college-vote-count-2021/h_d05427522929cd5a14c876b25d8872c9

21. Blitzer, Wolf. "The Trump insurrection: 24 hours that shook America," Twitter, January 10, 2021. https://twitter.com/wolfblitzer/status/1348264418086449157?s=20

22. Hosenball, Mark, and Lynch, Sarah N. "Exclusive: FBI finds scant evidence U.S. Capitol attack was coordinated—sources," Reuters, August 20,2021. https://www.reuters.com/world/us/exclusive-fbi-finds-scant-evidence-us-capitol-attack-was-coordinated-sources-2021-08-20/

23. De Luce, Dan. "Tucker Carlson says the NSA is spying on him. Is that even plausible? It's highly unlikely, but it's possible if the Fox host was speaking, knowingly or not, to foreigners under surveillance," NBC News, July 3, 2021, 6:00 AM EST. https://www.nbcnews.com/news/all/tucker-carlson-says-nsa-spying-him-even-plausible-n1272922

24. Herb, Jeremy. "NSA review finds no evidence supporting Tucker Carlson's claims NSA was spying on him, sources say," CNN Politics, July 24, 2021, 5:12 PM EST. https://www.cnn.com/2021/07/24/politics/nsa-review-tucker-carlson-spying-claims/index.html

25. Linge, Mary Kay. "Tucker Carlson's 'unmasking' claim confirmed by NSA investigators: report," *New York Post*, July 24, 2021, 5:38 PM EST. https://nypost.com/2021/07/24/tucker-carlsons-unmasking-claim-confirmed-by-nsa-investigators-report/

26. Barro, Robert J. "Bias beyond a reasonable doubt," *Weekly Standard* 10, no. 12 (December 2004): ProQuest page 14.

27. Prat, "Media power."

28. Groseclose, Tim, and Jeffrey Milyo. "A measure of media bias," *Quarterly Journal of Economics* 120, no. 4 (2005): 1191–1237. http://www.jstor.org/stable/25098770

29. Ibid.

30. Povich, Elaine S. *Partners & Adversaries: The Contentious Connection between Congress & the Media* (Arlington, VA: Freedom Forum, 1996).

31. Tierney, John. "Finding biases on the bus," *New York Times*, August 1, 2004. https://www.nytimes.com/2004/08/01/us/political-points.html

32. Brooks, David. "Ruling class war," *New York Times*, September 11, 2004. https://www.nytimes.com/2004/09/11/opinion/ruling-class-war.html

33. Groseclose and Milyo. "A measure of media bias."

34. "Unbiased and unloved," *Economist*, September 22, 2012, 72. The Economist Historical Archive, accessed August 2, 2021, www.link.gale.com/apps/doc/GP4100922970/ECON?u=usocal_main&sid=bookmark-ECON&xid=f469d2bd

35. Barr, Jeremy. "The new CNN is more opinionated and emotional. Can it still be 'The most trusted name in news'?" *Washington Post*, May 12, 2021, 6:00 AM EST. https://www.washingtonpost.com/lifestyle/media/cnn-opinionated-emotional-zucker/2021/05/11/5f32eb38-7f92-11eb-81db-b02f0398f49a_story.html

36. Ibid.

37. Ibid.

38. Fung, Katherine. "Who is Chris Wallace? Fox anchor, a registered Democrat, first asked Trump about presidential ambitions in 1988," *Newsweek*, September 29, 2020. https://www.newsweek.com/who-chris-wallace-fox-anchor-registered-democrat-first-asked-trump-about-presidential-1534649

39. Vogels, Emily A., Perrin, Andrew, and Anderson, Monica. "Most Americans think social media sites censor political viewpoints," PEW Research Center, released August 19, 2020. www.pewresearch.org

40. Lopez, German. "Donald Trump's long history of racism, from the 1970s to 2020," Vox, August 13, 2020, 7:00 PM EST. https://www.vox.com/2016/7/25/12270880/donald-trump-racist-racism-history

41. Stolberg, Sheryl Gay, and Herndon, Astead W. "'Lock the S.O.B.s up': Joe Biden and the era of mass incarceration," *New York Times*, June 25, 2019. https://www.nytimes.com/2019/06/25/us/joe-biden-crime-laws.html

42. C-SPAN. "Sen. Biden—Full speech in support of the Biden Hatch Crime Bill—November 18, 1993," C-SPAN User-Created Clip, December 8, 2019. https://www.c-span.org/video/?c4811303/user-clip-joe-biden

43. Stolberg and Herndon. "'Lock the S.O.B.s up.'"

44. Gadsden, Brett. "Here's how deep Biden's busing problem runs," Politico, May 5, 2019. https://www.politico.com/magazine/story/2019/05/05/joe-biden-busing-problem-226791/

45. Gass, Nick. "The 15 most offensive things that have come out of Trump's mouth." Politico, December 8, 2015, 10:21 PM EST. https://www.politico.eu/article/15-most-offensive-things-trump-campaign-feminism-migration-racism/

46. Saunders, Debra. "Harry Reid's gaffes just keep on coming," *San Francisco Chronicle*, August 26, 2014, 1:41 PM EST. https://www.indystar.com/story/opinion/2014/08/26/harry-reids-gaffes-just-keep-coming/14628749/

47. Bynum, Bill. "Black skin," *The Lancet* 360, no. 9329 (July 2002): 346. https://doi.org/10.1016/S0140-6736(02)09543-0

48. Holland, Steve. "Senate's Reid tells Obama he regrets racial remarks," Reuters, January 9, 2010, 2:03 PM EST. https://www.reuters.com/article/us-obama-reid-apology/senates-reid-tells-obama-he-regrets-racial-remarks-idUSTRE6081V820100109

49. Gillispie, Brandon. "MSNBC panel defends 'Uncle Tim' slur, suggests Tim Scott 'doesn't know what racism is,'" Fox News, April 30, 2021. https://www.foxnews.com/media/msnbc-uncle-tim-hashtag-slur-racism; Moore, Mark. "Twitter allows 'Uncle Tom' to trend for hours after Sen. Tim Scott's rebuttal, and then took action," *New York Post*, April 29, 2021. https://nypost.com/2021/04/29/sen-tim-scott-attacked-as-uncle-tim-on-twitter-after-gop-rebuttal/

50. Chasmar, Jessica. "Dr. Ben Carson fights back against 'Uncle Tom' attack," *Washington Times*, March 27, 2013. https://www.washingtontimes.com/news/2013/mar/27/dr-ben-carson-fights-back-against-uncle-tom-attack/

51. Smith, Kyle. "Media ignore racial attack on Larry Elder because he's a black Republican," *Washington Times*, September 9, 2021. https://nypost.com/2021/09/09/media-ignore-racial-attack-on-larry-elder-because-hes-republican/

52. Riley, Jason L. "Behind the elite hatred of Clarence Thomas," *Wall Street Journal*, November 17, 2020, 6:00 PM EST. https://www.wsj.com/articles/behind-the-elite-hatred-of-clarence-thomas-11605654039

53. Short, Philip. *Banda*. (London: Routledge & Kegan Paul, 1974).

54. Ibid.

55. Mastrangelo, Dominick. "Megyn Kelly: Media's portrayal of Jan. 6 'so much worse than it actually was,'" *The Hill*, July 13, 2021, 9:42 AM EST. https://thehill.com/homenews/media/562683-megyn-kelly-medias-portrayal-of-jan-6-so-much-worse-than-it-really-was; Wagner et al. "Jake Tapper: 'We're watching an attempt at sedition.'"

56. Alverez, M., Cheibub, J. A., Limongi, F., and Przeworski, A. "Classifying political regimes," *Studies in Comparative International Development* 31, no. 2 (Summer 1996): 3–36

57. Itkowitz, Colby. "Hillary Clinton: Trump is an 'illegitimate president,'" *Washington Post*, September 26, 2019. https://www.washingtonpost.com/politics/hillary-clinton-trump-is-an-illegitimate-president/2019/09/26/29195d5a-e099-11e9-b199-f638bf2c340f_story.html

58. Krieg, Gregory. "Police injured, more than 200 arrested at Trump inauguration protests in DC," CNN, January 21, 2017. https://www.cnn.com/2017/01/19/politics/trump-inauguration-protests-womens-march/index.html

59. Goldberg, Bernard. "It's no surprise that Americans don't trust a biased news media," *The Hill*, August 31, 2020, 10:00 AM EDT. https://thehill.com/opinion/white-house/513945-its-no-surprise-that-americans-dont-trust-a-biased-news-media

60. "Gallup/Knight Poll: Americans' concerns about media bias deepen, even as they see it as vital for democracy," Knight Foundation, August 4, 2020. https://knightfoundation.org/press/releases/gallup-knight-poll-americans-concerns-about-media-bias-deepen-even-as-they-see-it-as-vital-for-democracy/

61. Edmonds, Rick. "US ranks last among 46 countries in trust in media, Reuters Institute report finds," Poynter, June 24, 2021. https://www.poynter.org/ethics-trust/2021/us-ranks-last-among-46-countries-in-trust-in-media-reuters-institute-report-finds/

62. Sevenzo, Farai. "Bedtime for Banda," Transition 2000, no. 85 (2000): 4–29. https://www.jstor.org/stable/3137481

63.Sam Mpasu. *Political Prisoner 3/75* (Balaka: Montford Press, 1995), 152.

64. Ezrow, Natasha, and Frantz, Erica. *Dictators and Dictatorships* (New York: Continuum, 2011), 19–23.

65. Geddes, Barbara. *Paradigms and Sand Castles: Theory Building and Research Design in Comparative Politics* (Analytical Perspectives on Politics) (Ann Arbor: University of Michigan Press, 2003).

66. Ezrow and Frantz. *Dictators and Dictatorships.*

67. Ibid.

68. Ibid.

69. Ibid.

70. Bollen, Kenneth A. "Issues in the Comparative Measurement of Political Democracy," *American Sociological Review* 45, no. 3 (1980): 370–90. https://doi.org/10.2307/2095172

71. "Supporting free and fair elections," USAID. https://2012-2017.usaid.gov/what-we-do/democracy-human-rights-and-governance/supporting-free-and-fair-elections

72. Ibid.

73. *Boston Herald* Editorial Staff. "Mainstream media's silence on Biden story scandalous," *Boston Herald*, October 16, 2020. https://www.bostonherald.com/2020/10/16/mainstream-medias-silence-on-biden-story-scandalous/

74. Spangler, Todd. "Twitter still blocking a NY Post story based on alleged Hunter Biden emails, Newspaper's account remains frozen," *Variety*, October 17, 2020. https://variety.com/2020/digital/news/twitter-blocking-nypost-china-hunter-biden-account-locked-1234808416/

75. Staff Writer. "S Africa praises Zimbabwe elections," Reuters, April 2, 2005. https://www.aljazeera.com/news/2005/4/2/s-africa-praises-zimbabwe-elections; Kelto, Anders. "In Zimbabwe's media, it's all about Robert Mugabe," NPR, May 13, 2012. https://www.npr.org/2012/05/13/152521669/in-zimbabwes-media-its-all-about-robert-mugabe

76. Ezrow and Frantz. *Dictators and Dictatorships*, 216.

77. Short. *Banda*, 253.

78. Quist-Arcton, Ofeibea. "Robert Mugabe, veteran president of Zimbabwe, dead at 95," NPR, September 6, 2019, 1:17 AM EST. https://www.npr.org/2019/09/06/377714687/robert-mugabe-veteran-president-of-zimbabwe-dead-at-95

79. Crwys-Williams, Jennifer. *Dictionary of South African Quotations* (London: Penguin Books, 1994), 53.

Chapter 2

Political Correctness

Speaking to spouses of African presidents, former US first lady Michelle Obama said, "We cannot waste the spotlight, it is temporary; and life is short; and change is needed; and women are smarter than men."[1]

If Mrs. Obama was not joking and was really on a crusade to convince the world that one gender—women—is better than the other, then she has already gotten one convert, her husband.

In a speech in 2019 in Singapore, the former president himself declared that "women are better than men," and that "if every nation on earth was run by women, you would see a significant improvement across the board on just about everything . . . living standards and outcomes."[2]

Neither Mr. Obama nor his wife gave any data or scientific proof to support their point. To date, all credible scientific studies seem to suggest no difference in intelligence between the sexes.

Nevertheless, when the former first family made their claim, their respective audiences gave them thunderous handclapping approval and a lot of laughter. The audiences clearly knew there is no scientific data or theories out there to prove this claim. But they still went ahead and approved of it.

Suppose for a moment, Mr. and Mrs. Obama had claimed that men, not women, are the ones who are more intelligent and make better leaders, would their respective audiences have given the same thunderous approval?

The Obamas probably would have been booed off stage and subjected to negative press coverage. Yet this latter claim would have been just as equally false as the former, which was welcomed by the audience.

Even scientists are, sometimes, vulnerable to this tendency to want to believe that women are better. Consider a *New York Times* column by Nicholas Kristof titled, "What the Pandemic Reveals about the Male Ego." The article appeared on June 13, 2020, in the early months of the coronavirus pandemic.

In the article, Kristof claims that he "compiled death rates from the coronavirus for 21 countries around the world, 13 led by men and eight by women.

The male-led countries suffered an average of 214 coronavirus-related deaths per million inhabitants. Those led by women lost only one-fifth as many, 36 per million."

Kristof then concludes, "If the United States had the coronavirus death rate of the average female-led country, 102,000 American lives would have been saved out of the 114,000 lost."

From a scientific point of view, Kristof's analysis of the data is very poor. One would forgive him because he is neither a scientist nor a data analyst. His analysis did not consider crucial parameters like the size of the countries, the countries' geographical positions, the total number of women leaders in the world versus total number of male leaders in the word, and of course, the fact that that not all of the countries that did not do well with the virus were led by men. Although he mentions this last factor, he does not use it in his analysis.

Kristof's article is also based on a somewhat erroneous concept, prevalent in the media in the early days of the pandemic, that the coronavirus's devastation of a country was largely dependent on the country's response to the pandemic, that if a leader of the country acted in a certain way, then his country would be spared. In those early days of the pandemic, there were models that appeared to back this suggestion.

However, the world now knows that there was not much scientific backing to this claim, and most of those early models were not even robust enough to have been used for those predictions.

The most surprising thing about Kristof's article is that, in spite of the flawed nature of his analysis, there were scientists who agreed with his reasoning. He quotes them in the article.

One would have expected that scientists would have been cautious at the time, especially since this was just about four months into the pandemic, and there was limited data and knowledge about it.

Nevertheless, those scientists went ahead and gave their opinion in support of the article. Dr. Ezekiel Emanuel of the University of Pennsylvania said: "We often joke that men drivers never ask for directions. I actually think there's something to that also in terms of women's leadership, in terms of recognizing expertise and asking experts for advice, and men sort of barreling ahead like they got it."

Professor Anne W. Rimoin of the University of California, Los Angeles, said, "Countries led by women do seem to be particularly successful in fighting the coronavirus. New Zealand, Denmark, Finland, Germany, Iceland, Norway have done so well perhaps due to the leadership and management styles attributed to their female leaders."

So, why was it so easy for these two scientists to endorse a half-baked scientific theory when it was in favor of women? Surely, they would not have endorsed any such half-baked scientific theory if it was in favor of men.

Also, why was it that the Obamas' audiences got animated and happy by the claim that women are better than men. Why is it that people generally clap hands when somebody says women are more intelligent but then get angry by the opposite claim?

What is the reason for this double standard?

The answer is simple: it is because of "political correctness." It is a philosophy in which society lies to itself and pretends to believe its own lies, with the hope that pretending to believe the lies will make the society a better place. It also sometimes represents the desire to cover up a very uncomfortable worldly truth by suppressing any mention of it.

A commentary in the feminist journal *Off Our Backs* defends political correctness and points out that the term *political correctness* means that people must be considerate of others beyond themselves, being inclusive rather than exclusive, and being ethical in behavior.[3]

However, others disagree. Libby Purves compares the phenomenon of political correctness to a screen that enforces the authority of the elite by literally preventing anybody from asking a clear question or getting a clear answer. He believes that the beginnings of political correctness were a sign of people trying to do right by one another, but now extreme examples have made it a laughingstock.[4]

Remember the times when political correctness was about dispelling unproven myths about other groups of people or gender? Those times are gone now as society wants to force the belief that certain previously disadvantaged groups are actually superior. As Purves put it, political correctness loses the plot when structures it sets up to protect the weak turn into structures to turn the weak into bullies, or when those structures force an epidemic of ridiculous historical apologies.[5]

Political correctness makes society feel good about itself. It makes the weak feel powerful, the average feel beautiful, and the mediocre feel intelligent, and gives excuses to the irresponsible. It really becomes a mask behind which all sorts of really damaging laziness, prejudice, and hostility can hide.[6]

Because of this numbing quality, political correctness is often a tool of choice used by those who want to control the masses.

The media uses political correctness, as a weapon of choice, to persuade citizens to vote for certain candidates they would not have voted for in an election or to support certain causes they would not have otherwise supported.

The most dangerous thing about political correctness is that it forces society to believe untruths and therefore prevents society from addressing the underlying problems directly. Problems that could easily have been solved now linger longer and even threaten to destroy the world, simply because society chose to believe untruths and thus could not solve them. No problem can be solved without first understanding it and accepting the truth about it.

Political correctness strikes directly at one of the fundamental pillars of modern civilization—the pursuit of truth. Scientific and technological advancement cannot flourish in a society that chooses to believe lies instead of the truth.

While the media's motive in advancing these ideas is to consolidate power, these false ideas make the real underlying society problems impossible to solve.

This chapter outlines some of the false ideas advanced by the media through political correctness.

One of those false ideas advanced by political correctness is the notion that socially diverse groups or teams are the most talented. Politicians, diversity advocates, and nongovernmental organizations have promoted the idea that social diversity brings creativity and talent into the workforce. Some have even gone as far as to mandate drastic affirmative action programs based on this idea.

The Southern Africa Development Community (SADC) is a southern African regional economic community comprising sixteen member states. One of its pet projects is a protocol on gender and development that calls for the sixteen southern African nations to take drastic actions to achieve gender equality and equity in all areas.[7]

Article 12 of the protocol says that the southern African governments shall endeavor that "at least 50% of decision-making position in the public and private are held by women," ensured by using affirmative action measures.[8]

That means that in any public or private workplace, there will be at least 50 percent women. And if the CEO or director is a man, the deputy CEO or deputy director should be a woman, and vice versa. This concept is generally known in the southern Africa region as "Gender 50-50."

SADC comprises sixteen southern African countries, namely, Angola, Botswana, Comoros, Democratic Republic of Congo (DRC), Eswatini, Lesotho, Madagascar, Malawi, Mauritius, Mozambique, Namibia, South Africa, Tanzania, Zambia, and Zimbabwe. These nations believe that by implementing Gender 50-50, they will spur creativity and innovation that will jump-start the economy of the region.

The world over, other than in the SADC region, there are many other examples of major local, regional, or global decisions made based on this idea that social diversity results in creativity and innovation. The idea has become universally accepted, even though there is not much proof for it. It is also an example of how political correctness can have negative consequences for a society, way of life, and eventually the whole of civilization.

The question of whether socially diverse teams are more creative or productive is important because it directly affects the advancement and economic well-being of society.

Take a manager of a corporation, as an example. If the manager buys into the idea that diverse teams lead to more creativity and productivity, he will spend more resources and time on building diverse teams. However, if diverse teams do not necessarily lead to more creativity and productivity, this manager will end up losing the company money, resources, and better talent—the talent he overlooked while pursuing diversity. In the long run, advancement of the industry will be curtailed. Since advances in the industry are instrumental to the advancement and sustainment of civilization, the manager's action will eventually negatively affect civilization.

Most importantly, by taking actions that result in less productivity and value for the company, the manager would effectively be imposing an unjust tax on his stockholders. It is not his responsibility to impose a tax on stockholders. As Milton Freedman puts it, imposition of taxes is a function of government—not an unelected individual like this manager.[9] It is therefore important to really find out if there is any to truth to the idea that socially diverse groups or teams more talented, and hence better performing.

Mathematically, the claim that perfectly gender or racially diverse groups are the most talented appears to be an oxymoron. If nature does not respect gender or race (as we reasonably believe), and thus distributes a particular talent in society to a small group of people without regard to gender or race, then at any particular point in time, that group of talented people will not be perfectly gender or racially diverse. Therefore, at any particular point in time, any randomly selected group that is also perfectly gender or racially diverse is less likely to be the most talented. However, of course, over a long period of time, the total number of talented people may be perfectly diverse.

The key here is the assumption that the distribution of talent in society at any particular point in time does not depend on gender or race. Without that assumption, a different conclusion can be reached. This problem is akin to a common combinatorial problem,[10] where a large sample of unequal numbers of blue and red balls are placed in an urn, and the aim is to find the probability that randomly picking a few balls from the urn (X is the number of balls) will result in a small group comprising exactly half X blue balls and half X red balls.

In this analogy, the red and blue balls represent males and females in a society. Like gender as we believe it, the colors are just labels. They do not affect the physical composition or size of the balls in any way. The random picking of a few balls represents the random distribution of talent among a few people in the society without regard to gender.

Since nature is gender- or colorblind when it comes to distributing talent in a society, it is unlikely that any talent will be equally distributed among all genders and races at any particular point in time. Thus, teams or groups of people that are perfectly gender or racially diverse are less likely to be the most talented groups. In other words, when a company or organization is composed of perfectly socially diverse teams, mathematical logic tells us that the company or organization is less likely to be the most talented company.

This conclusion should not come as a surprise. Scientific studies conducted on the productivity of socially diverse groups have shown that social diversity does not necessarily improve efficiency or productivity at the workplace.

In describing group or team diversity, social scientists usually talk of three broad kinds of diversity, namely, informational diversity, social category diversity, and value diversity.[11] *Informational diversity* describes differences in knowledge bases and perspectives exhibited by different members of a group. Such differences usually derive from the education, experience, and expertise of the members of the group.[12]

Social category diversity refers to differences that put people in different social categories such as such as race, gender, and ethnicity. Social category is what most people refer to when they talk about diversity. *Value diversity* refers to differences in how different group members perceive what the task, goal, target, or mission should be. This is an explosive kind of diversity in that it usually results in conflict.[13]

A 1999 study by social researchers Karen Jehn, Gregory Northcraft and Margaret Neale found that the only form of diversity that improved group performance at the workplace was informational diversity. Social category diversity and values diversity did not improve performance. Social category diversity only positively affected group morale, whereas values diversity negatively impacted the group.[14]

In trying to understand the value of diversity, Katherine Y. Williams and Charles A. O'Reilly III reviewed over eighty studies on the effects of demography as it applies to management and organizations. These two researchers concluded that the preponderance of evidence of empirical evidence suggests that diversity is more likely to impede group functioning, and that diversity by itself is more likely to have negative than positive effects on group performance.[15] Not only does too much emphasis on diversity fail to improve performance and creativity, but it also actually reduces performance.

Another way to test the veracity of the claim that socially diverse teams are the most talented and productive teams is to look at the impact of social diversity at the national level. If social diversity of teams really enhanced creativity and productivity, then countries that embraced social diversity in government, civil, and private sectors would emerge as the most creative and productive countries, and by extension, the richest and most powerful countries.

One of the most readily available diversity data points for all countries is the record of gender diversity of lawmakers in national lawmaking houses. The Inter-Parliamentary Union (IPU) collects data on the proportion of seats held by women in national parliaments.[16] So, does this data show any relationship between social diversity in government and the nation's prosperity?

According to *US News and World Report*, the three most powerful nations on the planet are the United States, Russia, and China.[17] It is quite surprising to note how very poorly these three most powerful countries of the world do in terms of gender diversity in national parliaments.

In 2020, data from the IPU showed that only 24 percent of national lawmakers in China were women. This put China at number 72 on the list of the most gender-balanced lawmaking houses in the world. In the same year, in the United States, women made up 23.9 percent of Congress, putting it at number 76 in the world. Russia was at number 130, with only 15.8 percent of representation by women.

On top of that, of the three nations, only the United States has had a woman presiding over a national house/parliament; and this has only happened as recently as 2007. China and Russia have never had a woman as presiding officer over their national assemblies.

The United States, Russia, and China are not just the most powerful nations in the world, they are also among the twelve most-patent-generating countries of the world.[18] In other words, these three countries are among the most creative in the world. The other nine most-patent-generating countries are: Japan, the Republic of Korea, France, the UK, Italy, India, Switzerland, and the Islamic Republic of Iran.

How do these nine other most creative countries fare on parliamentary social diversity?

Germany is at number 47 with 30.9 percent of representation by women. Japan is number 164, with only 11.2 percent; South Korea is number 120, with only 17.1 percent; France is number 17, with 37.9 percent; the UK is number 39, with 32 percent; Italy is number 31, with 35.7 percent; India is number 148, with 12.6 percent; Switzerland is number 37, with 32.5 percent, and the Islamic Republic of Iran is number 179, with only 5.9 percent representation by women.

None of these 12 nations made the top-20 list of countries with the most gender diverse parliaments. In fact, it's the poor African countries of Mozambique, Senegal, Ethiopia, Namibia, and Rwanda that are in the top 20 on the list. The poor Caribbean nation of Cuba has a perfect gender balance in its parliament.

Certainly, if social diversity increased creativity and productivity, these poor countries would not be where they are now. They would have been more prosperous and scientifically advanced. Instead, it is China—one of the least diversity-tolerating nations of the world—that is on the robust upward developmental trajectory.

China's record on social diversity is quite dismal. First, there is not much racial diversity in China. China has the smallest share of migrants of any country in the world.[19] Second, China's record on gender diversity is not good. Hillary Clinton famously declared at the Beijing United Nations Fourth World Conference on Women that women's rights are human rights, a statement seen as a jab at the host nation's record.[20] She has since constantly spoken out against China's record on gender.[21]

Some Chinese academic programs accept only men or cap the number of female applicants. In some university entrance examinations, men are favored even if they score lower. Women are also heavily discriminated against in police and military recruitment. China is so concerned with what it calls "masculinity crisis among young Chinese men" that some institutions started offering free male-only kindergarten education to remedy the "crisis."[22]

In response to complaints of feminization of teenage boys in China, the Ministry of Education suggested propping up physical education and mental health classes in schools as measures to promote masculinity among boys. Feminization of boys is regarded as so dangerous that will imperil the survival of the nation if not cured.[23]

Traditionally, in China, the pursuit of a career and the possibility of a high position in society was a man's job. Men were likened to the pillar or backbone of the family.[24] Although women face many barriers to leadership the world over, Chinese women's barriers are said to be distinct.

Researchers Jiayi Zhao and Karen Jones postulated that these unique barriers could be a result of traditional Confucianism, which required a woman to obey the men in her life: obeying the father before marriage, obeying the husband during marriage, and obeying sons in widowhood.[25] Women were expected to aspire to the virtues of physical charm, fidelity, propriety in speech, and efficiency in needlework.[26]

Relatively few women in China progress to senior leadership in spite of the fact that there are many women in the labor force.[27] Employment rates of women in China are one of the highest in the world.[28] In Chinese educational institutions, only about 4.5 percent of Mainland China's higher education institution leaders are female.[29]

Despite its record on social diversity, China's growth in scientific, economic, and military power is unprecedented. In a short period of time, the Chinese have built revolutionary bullet trains, orbited the moon, constructed their own space station, and developed military technologies for disabling enemy satellites in orbits.

In 2021, the Chinese caught the world by surprise when they successful tested highly advanced, never seen before hypersonic missile technology. The US Joint Chiefs of Staff general Mark Milley referred to the event as something close to a Sputnik moment.[30] China's military transformation has been so fast that a top Pentagon official resigned in protest to what he perceived as America's inability to transform its military at the same rate as China.[31]

There are almost no credible peer-reviewed research studies that show that forms of diversity, other than diversity of thought, increase productivity. Of course, since this issue is politically charged, there is no shortage of studies or surveys that claim to demonstrate the benefits of diversity. Usually, these studies are not peer reviewed and are associated with political ideological groups, activists, or industries. And the researchers involved are usually not the traditional PhD researchers.

Take for instance, a study by the Boston Consultancy Group (BCG), which has widely been quoted in the media. The study claims to have found that "companies that reported above-average diversity on their management teams also reported innovation revenue that was 19 percentage points higher than that of companies with below-average leadership diversity—45% of total revenue versus just 26%."[32]

The study went on to claim that a hypothetical company of 50,000 employees and 1,500 people in management roles would increase its innovation by more than 1 percent if it made sure that at least 38 of those people in management were women. The same company would also increase its innovation by more than 1 percent if it simply made sure that 30 of the managers were from a different country from the company's.

From this, they conclude that diversity is very profitable to a company.

Obviously, these are big claims. As Rocio Lorenzo, the lead author of the report, put it, the results were warmly welcomed by the media and in some cases sensationalized.[33] Lorenzo also described herself as a person committed to diversifying the industry.

There is a catch in the report. The authors report that the study also looked at the effect of digitization on overall innovation and found that companies that place a greater emphasis on digital technology show a stronger correlation between diversity and innovation.[34]

The authors did not show why they believe that diversity alone seems to bring the claimed outcome when there was strong emphasis on digital technology. In fact, in a TED talk, Rocio Lorenzo, one of the authors, acknowledged that they did not know whether the companies with more socially diverse leaders could simply be companies that are already open to new ideas, and therefore more open to diversity, even though the diversity itself does not necessarily bring more innovation.[35] The study also did not address why some of the most innovative countries like China, Iran, and India do not necessarily have the most diverse leadership in the workforce.

It is also important to note that the authors of the study are not traditional PhD researchers who would normally pass their findings through a peer-review mechanism before publishing them. The four authors of the report were Rocio Lorenzo, Miki Tsusaka, Nicole Voigt, and Matt Krentz. Lorenzo is a lawyer, Tsusaka has a BA and MBA, Voigt is a civil engineer with an MBA, and Krentz has a BA and MBA.

The mechanics of ensuring diverse teams in a company are themselves just very problematic. Suppose a manager of a company wants to hire a topflight engineer. Normally the manager, with the help of human resources, puts out an advertisement for the job.

Suppose 30 people respond to the advertisement. This manager will have the opportunity of choosing a good engineer from among the 30 candidates. If he is not satisfied with the pool, he may decide to re-advertise the position. Assuming, 30 more people responds to this second advertisement, the manager now has a pool of 60 candidates to choose from.

The problem comes in when this manager decides beforehand that he has to hire a minority in this advertised position in order to make his group diverse. US laws do not allow him to indicate in the advertisement that only black people or Hispanics should apply. His only option is to put a vague statement that says "minority and women are encouraged to apply," which usually appears on all advertisements, anyway.

Out of the 30 applicants to the first advertisement, he may get maybe three black people. This is certainly not a good enough sample to pick a good engineer. So, what does he do? If he re-advertises the position, he may get three more black people. Now he has a sample of only six candidates to pick from. Still not a good sample, but the re-advertisement will probably have cost him time and resources.

The most reasonable thing for the manager to do is to just pick one of the first three he gets among the first 30 applicants. His odds do not really get that better with re-advertisement; he might as well not re-advertise. The result is a situation that, when a company has to hire a socially diverse person for a position, merit is usually put on the back burner. Unfortunately, this ends up just strengthening the erroneous perception that minorities are less capable.[36]

This situation would probably have been different if the manager had just advertised straight up that he was only looking to hire a minority for the job. That could have attracted a lot of minorities to apply, and therefore would have increased the pool of candidates to choose from.

This discussion does not mean that diversity is bad. Diversity makes people and nations feel good about themselves. A diverse society should be the goal of civilized society. However, it is wrong to use untruths to advance a cause, however, just.

Another myth advanced by political correctness is the idea that affirmative action is victimless. Affirmative action refers to a set of practices undertaken by employers, university admissions offices, and government agencies to go beyond nondiscrimination, with the goal of actively improving the economic status of minorities and women with regard to employment, education, and business ownership and growth.[37]

On paper, affirmative action should help to offset the systematic barriers that minorities and women continue to face in pursuing education and employment opportunities.[38] Data, however, tells a different story. Affirmation action has real victims and does not always equalize opportunities in society. In fact, it leaves some of the underrepresented groups in a worse position.

Consider for instance the number of directors on the boards of Fortune 100 companies. In 2018, white men had the largest representation in Fortune 100 boardrooms. The top three representations were 750 white men, 234 white women, and 94 black men.[39]

As companies moved to diversify the boardroom, there was a huge increase in the number of women and a somehow inexplicable drop in the number of black men. According to Deloitte, just between 2018 and 2020, the number of white women increased by 15 percent (gained 34 more seats); the number of black women increased by over 14 percent (gained 6 more seats), while the number of black men dropped by 1 percent (lost 1 seat).[40]

Given that affirmative action is intended to make white men share opportunities with minorities and women, it is understandable that the number of white men in Fortune 100 company boardrooms dropped during the same period. What is inexplicable is why representation by black men declined. After all, the total number of black men in Fortune 100 boardrooms is only one-third of that of white women. What is the reason for this decline? Does America have more than enough black men in boardrooms?

In fact, the situation is even worse in Fortune 500 boardrooms. During the same period, 2018 and 2020, over 200 white women and 29 black women were added to the boardrooms while the number of black men was reduced by 5. As of October 2021, of the 11 black board members in the top 10 Fortune 500 companies, only four were black men, and the remaining seven were black women.

Even in the tech world, where you have a disproportionately large number of black men relative to black women, black board members are overwhelmingly women. It certainly cannot be because of lack of black men with expertise in STEM. American schools have always graduated more black men than black women in STEM fields. In the 2017–2018 academic year alone, 31,802 black men and 19,458 black women graduated with STEM degrees.[41] Just as among all the other racial groups, more black women than black men graduate in all fields of study other than STEM.[42]

In America, the black man bears the brunt of racism against black people. He has a higher high school dropout rate than black women,[43] is incarcerated at the highest rate,[44] and is more likely to be misunderstood by law enforcement. Yet the black man even loses out even on programs meant to specifically help him. In the aftermath of the death of George Floyd at the hands of law enforcement, most companies resolved to diversify their leadership workforce. The prevailing narrative at the time was that black men in America are so negatively stereotyped that people, including law enforcement, look at them as nothing more than an unnecessary threat. Companies wanted to hire deserving black people to their leadership teams to counter this stereotype.

One would think that, based on this logic, these companies would have been hiring black men. That is not what happened. Although the number of black people appointed to boards of Russell 3000 companies jumped in the aftermath of George Floyd's death,[45] it is interesting to note that of the 21 black people appointed by companies that did not have a black director before Floyd's death, only seven were black men, and the remaining 14 were black women. One can argue that these numbers in themselves enhance rather than diminish the negative image of black men.

The tendency to overlook black men in favor of black women first, and women generally, is a common occurrence not just in boardrooms but across all levels of corporate America. Black men are overlooked partly because gender equality is more politically correct than racial equality, and partly because employing black women fills two quotas: gender and race. And, for those who have always been uncomfortable with black men, hiring a black woman represents an opportunity to claim racial diversity without necessarily having to deal with the black man.

So affirmative action, a system that was really intended to level the playing field by replacing white men with deserving minorities and women, is now clearly hurting black men. Black men, the very group of people affirmative action is supposed to help the most, are victims of affirmative action.

Nobody knows exactly how these negative consequences of affirmative action on black men affect the black community in general. Perhaps some of the ills in the black community, such as the skyrocketing of-out-of-wedlock births, could be tied to this systematic segregation of black men. Perhaps the broken African American family institution is a direct result of systematic segregation of black men.

This appears to be what Robert J. Willis predicted in a 1999 paper titled "A Theory of Out-of-Wedlock Childbearing." He postulated that in a society where females are in excess supply and have sufficiently high incomes, a marriage-market equilibrium may exist in which children are born within marriage to high-income parents, whereas in low-income groups, men father children by multiple partners outside of marriage.[46]

Clearly, black men are victims of affirmative action, and the claim that affirmative action has only an upside is false.

Another version of this false idea is the argument that strong affirmative action programs will help a country develop faster and move away from poverty. In reality, it is difficult to find a country in the world that was poor before and then became rich solely or mostly because it implemented heavy affirmative action programs. There are, however, several countries that went off the rails after implementing strong affirmative action programs. South Africa is a good example.

Until the early 1990s, South Africa was under a system of government known as apartheid. The brutal apartheid systematically segregated non-whites South Africans. It resulted in the confining of black males to only certain parts of the country, a mediocre education system for the black and mixed-race minority, and denial of some basic human rights.

The end of apartheid culminated in the election of the famed anti-apartheid hero, Nelson Mandela, as the first black president. During that election, the question in South Africa was always how to integrate the largely poorly edu-cated nonwhite majority into the economy and government affairs that had thus far been dominated by only the white minority. In a famous televised pre-election debate between Nelson Mandela and the then-president F. W. de Klerk, the candidates attacked each other's plans for integrating all races into the economy of South Africa.[47]

In response to journalist Ferial Haffajee's question, Mandela described his plan for building houses for the masses and providing jobs, free quality edu-cation, and hospital services, all paid for by rearranging the budget, which he believed spent too much on arms.

When de Klerk pointed out that Mandela's plan was too ambitious and unworkable, and accused Mandela's party of using internationally discredited policies that would not attract investment, Mandela shot back by accusing de Klerk of being a man "not used to addressing the basic needs of the majority of the population, whose government is committed to a small minority."

De Klerk famously replied, "Let me say Mr. Mandela, my comments were not the comments of a man who is less than candid. They were the com-ments of somebody with experience; of somebody who sat in cabinet and worked through budgets since 1978 and who knows how the economy of the state works."

Nelson Mandela went on to win that election, and his party, the African National Congress (ANC), has been in power since then. The ANC worked hard to bring the black majority into the government and economy. However, the problem was that, because of apartheid, many black people were not qualified to integrate properly in the economy. During apartheid, black people had been denied a quality education and many other opportunities for advancement.

The ANC's answer to this lack of black qualified manpower was to simply get mostly unqualified faithful ANC members in positions to run the economy. Integration was much more important than merit. After all, there was a very good reason why blacks were not as qualified as white people. Thus, the government implemented aggressive affirmative action through programs like Black Economic Empowerment (BEE) and gender empowerment.

The results have not been very good. The South Africa of today is not economically and scientifically as powerful as the South Africa of fifty years ago. The South Africa of today is not associated with the same achievements of fifty years ago. The South Africa of these two different eras makes different international headlines.

Consider this: on December 3, 1967, a group of doctors, nurses, and technicians led by Dr. Christiaan Barnard performed the world's first-ever human-to-human heart transplant at Groote Schuur Hospital in Cape Town, South Africa. The news of this marvelous achievement spread around the world like wildfire. The *New York Times* of the next day, December 4, memorialized this event perfectly with a front-page headline, "Heart Transplant Keeps Man Alive in South Africa; Heart Transplanted from a Dead Woman and Started by Shock Is Keeping Man Alive in South Africa."[48]

The marvelous achievement by Dr. Barnard's team was not a mistake, neither was it unique in the South Africa of the time. The South African government had invested heavily in scientific research and technological infrastructure. This investment resulted in world-class research laboratories and scientists. In the following years, South Africa would go on to manufacture world-class cars, build a world-class university education, make many discoveries in science and technology—and, yes, even toy around with the idea of nuclear weapons.

The headlines in the South Africa of today are vastly different. Realities in the present South Africa are sobering. Corruption is so high that a former president has had to go to prison. The once mighty South African Airways (SAA), which extended its tentacles around the world, is dealing with the effects of a humiliating bankruptcy. The state power utility Eskom Holding SOC, Ltd. is in deep debt. The number of South African welfare recipients has ballooned sixfold since the end of apartheid. The BEE has resulted in creating a few black millionaires among the political elite while leaving millions of people still in poverty.[49]

South Africa took radical affirmative action initiatives with the aim of improving the country's welfare. In the end, the citizens—who were supposed to be benefactors of the system—have become the ultimate victims of affirmative action.

This discussion in no way claims that apartheid was good. Apartheid was an evil and oppressive system that was rightly ended. Affirmative action by the South African government was an honest initiative intended to right the wrongs of apartheid. Unfortunately, the truth is that there is no evidence that racial, tribal, or gender affirmative action initiatives lead to economic prosperity.

Another politically correct argument that is often put forward is the claim that kids perform poorly in school when they come from poorer households. This popular argument is often quoted in powerful political circles to explain away below-standard performance of minority kids, especially in the inner cities.

While the economic status of parents can affect kids' performance, what is usually not mentioned is that poverty does not seem to affect the academic performance of poor immigrant kids from poor African countries and the developing world. A 1994 study found that Africans were the most educated immigrant group in the United States.[50] And, according to the *Financial Times*, "Nigerians are the most highly educated of all groups, with 61 per cent holding at least a bachelor's degree compared with 31 per cent of the total foreign-born population and 32 per cent of the US-born population."[51]

A more interesting phenomenon is the fact that, in most African nations, poor kids perform just as well as rich kids. A study of learning inequality in ten francophone countries found little or no difference between children from different social origins who attended the same school. The performance of poor and rich kids attending the same school was almost identical. The economic status of the parents did not come into play.[52]

In a 1970s study published in the *Comparative Educational Review*, Stephen P. Heyneman observed that there was no relationship between socioeconomic status and test performance among Ugandan primary school children.[53] Heyneman concluded that, in Uganda, academic advantage was not an inevitable condition of economic privilege, and that poor but confident students were not handicapped by poverty.[54]

In poor developing countries, education is usually seen as the only gateway to success in life. There are few to none other options that poor people can use to change their economic status. Thus, poor kids take education as their only chance for a better life.[55]

For nearly forty years after independence, the country of Malawi had only one university and about thirty secondary schools. Almost all of these institutions were owned and run by the Malawi government. At about the age of thirteen, students would take primary school "leaving examinations," to compete for Form 1 places in the twenty-four secondary schools.

All students, coming from the poorest rural primary schools to the richest urban ones, sat for identical examinations at the same time. The examination was provided and proctored by the government. A total of about 80,000 students were essentially competing for 8,000 places. After another four years of secondary school, the students would take another government-proctored examination to compete for places in the country's single university—the University of Malawi.

In all of these examinations, it was very common to see poor kids from rural school performing just as well as or even better than rich kids from urban schools.

In one of his opinion pieces, *New York Times* columnist Nicholas Kristof writes about Angeline Mugwendere, a poor Zimbabwean girl who was "mocked by classmates because she traipsed to school barefoot in a torn dress with nothing underneath. She couldn't afford school supplies, so she would wash dishes for her teachers in hopes of being given a pen or paper in thanks."[56] Yet Angeline ended up getting the highest score in her district in the sixth-grade graduation examination.

So the popular idea that kids perform poorly in school when they come from poorer households could simply be a myth. It deliberately ignores other politically incorrect factors that affect the academic performance of American minority kids. Political correctness views complex problem in a simplistic way in order to make those problems comfortable for people. In the process, however, it misfocuses society and makes those problems harder to solve.

Consider the problem of low enrollment and high dropout rates for young girls in primary schools in Malawi in the early 1990s. At the time, the Malawi school system was divided into three sectors: primary schools, secondary schools, and the University of Malawi.

The primary school was the first school Malawian kids entered. Due to poor economic conditions, there were no kindergartens. Kids would stay at home until they were five or six years old before entering primary school. Primary school ran from Standard 1 to Standard 8. Secondary school ran from Form 1 to Form 4, and from there the students would be selected to attend the University of Malawi.

Given the low enrollment and high dropout rates for girls in the primary school, the United States Agency for International Development (USAID) wanted to help. To the Americans, the problem was simple: girls dropped out because older men were enticing them with money and impregnating them in the process. After, all this was Africa, where according to Western stereotypes, men heavily controlled women.

To solve the problem, USAID established and funded a program called Girls' Attainment in Basic Literacy and Education (GABLE). GABLE I and II ran from 1991 to 1998.[57] The main objective of GABLE was to increase girls' attendance and successful completion of the eight years of primary education. GABLE was to achieve this goal by removing what were believed to be the cultural barriers that prevented girls from advancing.[58]

These initiatives included giving all girls scholarships and financial assistance for school materials and basic needs. This was intended to counter what GABLE believed was society's reluctance to pay school fees for a girl child, and older men's tendencies to entice young girls with money. The program did not help boys, except indirectly through shared facilities such as a classroom, if GABLE built one, for instance. Otherwise, boys still paid all the school fees and did not receive any financial assistance.

On the radio, GABLE administrators and sponsors went further with bizarre allegations. They described Malawi culture as a culture where people do not believe in investing money in school fees for girls. They also alleged that giving the girls pocket money would deter them from having relationships with much older men that resulted in their getting pregnant and dropping out of school. They, however, did not support these accusations with data.

As with most US aid to developing nations, there is usually a tendency to claim progress even if the results appear otherwise. GABLE was not an exception. The final progress report gave flying colors to the program. However, hidden in those reports were disturbing truths. First, most of the progress reports were based on document analysis, but with no data collection on the ground. Most of the documents involved in the project were either missing or misplaced and "no financial information could be obtained that would allow for a better understanding of the link between specific financial input and the intended quality of educational outcome."[59]

The most interesting aspect of the project, however, was buried somewhere in the reports. While the free-for-girls schooling had encouraged many girls to enroll in primary schools, a significant number of these girls dropped out of school by the second half of primary school. From that perspective, GABLE failed to do what it was supposed to do. It failed to stem the dropout rate of girls in primary schools.[60]

Another surprising fact was that by the end of GABLE I, the quality and efficiency of primary education had become worse than when GABLE was first introduced. The administrators of GABLE claimed that this was due to the fact that GABLE had encouraged a lot of girls to enter the school system and therefore overwhelmed it. At the same time, they also claimed that the quality of school would have been worse without the introduction of GABLE.[61]

The very obvious contradiction between these two claims was not explained. Also, no data was given to support the assertion that school quality would have been worse without the introduction of GABLE, given that at the time GABLE I was introduced, there was no expectation that the quality of education would dip that low between 1991 and 1994.

In any case, the bottom line is that the claim that girls were dropping out simply because the culture did not condone paying for their educational expenses, or that they dropped out because sugar daddies enticed them with money for basic needs, proved to be wrong. Under GABLE, the girls had free school enrollment and had funding for their basic needs. Yet the basic problem of high dropout rates persisted.

The locals were not surprised. No average Malawian village parent was reluctant to pay his or her girl child's school fees, if the girl stayed in school. Securing school fees was difficult for both boys and girls. However, in a poor country where the much-desired social mobility is only achieved through education, parents are excited whenever their child, regardless of sex, excels in school. Also, most of those girls who dropped out of school because of pregnancies were impregnated by their peers.

The Americans had looked at the problem of high dropout rate for girls through the eyes of political correctness and ended up misdirecting resources to problems that were not an issue on the ground. By the end of the program, the high dropout rate for girls in the latter half of the primary school was still there.

This is just one of the many examples where the powerful force the world to look at a complex problem through a politically correct lens. There are many other examples. Sometimes the consequences of looking at problems through politically correct eyes can have devastating consequences.

In April 2014, a terrorist Islamist group in northern Nigeria known as Boko Haram kidnapped nearly two hundred girls from a boarding school. In a video released three weeks after the heinous act, the leader of Boko Haram, Abubakar Shekau claimed responsibility for the kidnappings and threatened to sell the girls, whom he referred to as slaves.[62]

In the video, Abubakar Shekau railed against Western education and demanded that all girls should leave school and get married. He warned that he would "give their hands in marriage because they are our slaves. We would marry them out at the age of 9. We would marry them out at the age of 12."[63]

To the Western media, the issue suddenly became a gender issue. The talking point was that Boko Haram had kidnapped and victimized the girls because all of Africa does not respect girls' education. *New York Times* columnist Nicholas Kristof wrote, "When terrorists in Nigeria organized a secret attack last month, they didn't target an army barracks, a police department or a drone base. No, Boko Haram militants attacked what is even scarier to a fanatic: a girls' school."[64]

"Why are fanatics so terrified of girls' education? Because there's no force more powerful to transform a society. The greatest threat to extremism isn't drones firing missiles, but girls reading books. In that sense, Boko Haram was behaving perfectly rationally—albeit barbarically—when it kidnapped some of the brightest, most ambitious girls in the region and announced plans to sell them as slaves. If you want to mire a nation in backwardness, manacle your daughters."[65]

In another article, Kristof argued that the "attack in Nigeria is part of a global backlash against girls' education by extremists. The Pakistani Taliban shot Malala Yousafzai in the head at age 15 because she advocated for girls' education. Extremists threw acid in the faces of girls walking to school in Afghanistan. And in Nigeria, militants destroyed 50 schools last year alone."[66]

Kristof also shared his opinion on social media and on television. Celebrities and politicians shared their views of the importance of girls' education and the need for societies to stop oppressing them.

In a Mother's Day address to the nation, first lady Michelle Obama, described the kidnappings as "a terrorist group determined to keep these girls from getting an education—grown men attempting to snuff out the aspirations of young girls."[67]

Mrs. Obama had earlier famously held an image of herself on Twitter carrying a placard that read that read "#BringBackOurGirls."[68] Later, at a function, Mrs. Obama said she did not understand why terrorists would be "so threatened by the prospect of girls going to school that they would break into a dormitory in the middle of the night."

Commenting on Michelle Obama's statement, BBC News White House correspondent Tara McKelvey wrote, "Most of the Nigerian girls she tried to save will never finish school. But because of her efforts, other children will."[69] In the same article, McKelvey appeared to blame boys when she wrote, "In order to show commitment to Boko Haram, boys attack their own families."[70]

Emily Gustafsson-Wright and Katie Smith of the Brookings Institution wrote an article about the kidnapped girls on April 17, 2014. In their article, Emily and Katie described the incident as the latest in the series of tragedies committed by Boko Haram. The group had killed over seventy in the Nigerian capital on the same day. In the previous year, the group had killed thirty teachers and destroyed many houses.

However, just like many media and political commentators, Gustafsson-Wright and Smith tie the kidnapping to gender issues and the inability to improve girls' education. "Girls, especially those in the north, are at a considerable disadvantage relative to their male counterparts—37 percent of primary-age girls in the rural northeast do not attend school, compared with 30 percent of boys," they wrote.

On May 21, 2014, the US Congress House Committee on Foreign Affairs held hearings on the topic "Boko Haram: The Growing Threat to Schoolgirls, Nigeria and Beyond." In his opening remarks, committee chairman Edward R. Royce (Democrat from California) said that the mission of Boko Haram was "to carry out a war against those who educate or empower women. And the greatest sin to them is not treating women as chattel, which they do, or enslaving women, which they purport to justify, or selling women. No. The greatest sin to them is to be involved in educating or teaching young women how to read and write."[71]

To the media, the activists, and the politicians, the kidnapping of the girls was simply a gender issue resulting from a culture of not valuing girls' education. Was that the correct assessment of the problem? Were the Boko Haram kidnappings of the two hundred Nigerian girls a gender issue?

Boko Haram is a northern-Nigerian-based radical terrorist group that seeks to overthrow the current Nigerian government and replace it with a government based on Islamic law. Their signature issue appears to be the brutal fight against Western education. In fact, the name "Boko Haram" means "Western education is evil or forbidden."

Before kidnapping the girls, Boko Haram had a familiar modus operandi when it came to terrorizing schools. Whenever they came to a school, they would tell all of the girls to go back home and get married. Then they would take the boys, lock them up in a building, and set the building on fire. The boys would be burned to death or shot dead. On that April 2014 night, there were no boys at that school, and they decided to kidnap the girls. This hardly sounds like an anti-girls' education campaign based on cultural beliefs that put women down.

The Boko Haram kidnappings were not a gender issue but rather a terrorism issue. Only two months earlier, Boko Haram had committed a gruesome atrocity involving boys only. The media knew this, but they chose to make the Boko Haram story a gender issue, possibly because it was politically correct to do so.

In fact, on February 24, 2014, the *New York Times* reported that "Boko Haram fatally burned or shot dozens of male students in an attack late Monday on a state college in northeastern Nigeria" and that none of the girls were reported to have been harmed.

"After the attackers separated the students, they told the women to read the Quran, go home and find husbands," the *New York Times* reported. The article further said a similar attack killed forty students at a nearby state school in September 2013. "Boko Haram," the article said, "deliberately targets state educational institutions as part of its Islamist, antisecular campaign."

Reuters covered the same story on February 26, 2014, reporting that the death toll had risen to fifty-nine. Apart from the students who had been burned to death, bodies with bullet wounds had been discovered in the bush after the students who had escaped died of their injuries. Reuters also confirmed that all victims were male students: "Fresh bodies have been brought in. More bodies were discovered in the bush after the students who had escaped with bullet wounds died from their injuries."

NBC news quoted a police commissioner who said, "All those killed were boys. No girls were touched." But the network also pointed out that "Boko Haram have also started abducting scores of girls, a new tactic reminiscent of Uganda's cult-like Lord's Resistance Army in decades past."

The Western media knew that the Boko Haram kidnapping of the two hundred girls was not a gender issue but a terrorism one. Boys had suffered equally or perhaps more than girls under the hands of Boko Haram. Yet the media decided to make the issue a gender problem, and in the process misdirected focus and resources. Perhaps it should not be surprising that the Boko Haram problem in northern Nigeria has still not been resolved.

Writer and activist Chitra Nagarajan accused the media of creating a hierarchy of humanity, with "some people being valued above others."

"We all know about the Chibok girls but how many of us know about the Buni Yadi boys? A few weeks before the abductions from Chibok, an estimated 59 boys were lined up in the Federal Government College in Buni Yadi, had knives drawn across their throat, were gunned down or burned alive. Seeing only women and girls as victims plays into gendered stereotypes that we must move away from. It also presents a highly distorted version of reality," Nagarajan wrote.

Robyn Dixon of the *Los Angeles Times* also pointed out the double standard. Commenting on the coverage of the kidnapped girls, she wrote, "But attention on the Chibok girls overlooked a string of attacks on Nigerian boys that began in 2013. Schoolboys and male college students have been locked into dormitories, burned alive, shot in their beds, blown up or had their throats cut—all for seeking an education."

A much more interesting aspect of the Boko Haram story is that before they kidnapped the girls, the Barak Obama administration had refused to designate Boko Haram as a terrorist organization in spite of all the boy-related atrocities attributed to the group. Even when Boko Haram bombed the UN headquarters in Abuja in 2011, the State Department refused to place Boko Haram on the list of foreign terrorist organizations, despite the urging of the Justice Department, the FBI, the CIA, and over a dozen senators and congressmen.[72]

While designating three Nigerians associated with Boko Haram as specially designated global terrorists (SDGT), the State Department stopped short of designating Boko Haram as a foreign terrorist organization (FTO).[73] The move disappointed security experts like Morgan Lorraine Roach, who warned the Obama administration not to take the threat posed by Boko Haram lightly.[74]

Another issue where political correctness has made a complex problem even more difficult to solve is that of genital mutilation. The dangers and horror of female genital mutilation have been well documented. There are many organizations fighting female genital mutilation. In fact, the United

Nations, and specifically UNFPA, jointly with UNICEF, have campaigns to end female genital mutilation.[75]

What is interesting about this debate is that nobody is allowed to talk about the dangers of male genital mutilation, or circumcision. It is highly politically incorrect to do so. Activists and some doctors angrily shut that debate down.

In an article in *Missouri Medicine*, Elizabeth Piontek and Justin Albani ridicule the idea of mentioning male and female genital mutilation in the same breath.[76] "It is absurd to equate the simple removal of the male foreskin for health reasons to the barbaric amputation of the female clitoris for the sole purpose of preventing the woman from experiencing pleasure during sex," they write.

Piontek and Albani argue that male circumcision has many benefits, and it is done on a newborn in a safe hospital environment, whereas female genital mutilation has no benefits, it traumatizes girls, and has many lifelong side effects. The problem Piontek, Albani, and many activists make is to equate female genital mutilation, as practiced in primitive communities, with male circumcision as practiced in advanced Western countries. In their article, Piontek and Albani appear to assume that all male circumcision is neonatal and properly performed by a trained and experienced operator. That is not the case.

In countries where female genital mutilation is performed, male genital mutilation is practiced not in the comfort of a hospital but in a bush camp. It is performed on boys, about twelve years of age, by abruptly cutting off a chunk of their foreskin using a blunt knife or razor. They are not allowed to even cry because this is supposed to be the rite of passage to manhood. Quite a number of these boys develop serious complications from these procedures. In 2013, in South Africa alone, eighty boys died from these procedures.[77]

Traditional male circumcision is widely practiced among the Xhosa tribe in South Africa. In 2005 and 2006, the Mthatha General Hospital alone recorded twenty-nine deaths of boys from complications due to the traditionally performed male circumcision.[78] A report by the South African Commission for the Promotion and Protection of the Rights of Cultural, Religious and Linguistic Communities reported that between 2008 and 2014, in the provinces of Eastern Cape and Limpopo alone, 419 boys died and 456,000 were hospitals for complications due to traditional male circumcision.[79]

Across the sub-Saharan region, millions of young boys pass through this ritual every year.[80] It is usually performed at a week-or month-long camp in the bush. No uncircumcised person or woman is allowed to visit or come near the camp unless they are going to be circumcised. If an uncircumcised person comes near the camp, he is abducted and forcibly circumcised. Everything learned in that camp is supposed to be a secret.

A person is considered a real man only after passing through this ritual. Women refuse to be in a relationship or marriage with any man who has not passed through the ritual. So, genital mutilation is another issue where political correctness is preventing a full solution to a complex problem.

The media uses political correctness to strengthen its own power. If poor minorities can continue to believe that their kids cannot do well in school because of their economic background, then they will most likely look to the media-favored politicians who claim to have a solution for helping these poor inner-city kids who cannot help themselves. In the process, the power of the media grows.

If minorities and underrepresented people continue to believe that affirmative action helps all minorities and underrepresented groups, then politicians will continue to have leverage over these people. Usually, these affirmative action–friendly politicians are also supported by the media. If minorities believe that there is no way they can advance except through diversity standards imposed by government, then minorities will continue to look to government as their savior.

If families in minority neighborhoods continue to weaken, forcing communities to depend more and more on the government, then the media and the politicians it supports will have increased their power over the minorities. The media fosters an environment where minorities embark on group-think and are afraid of being different.

Inevitably, because political correctness is not the truth, those who push politically correct ideals on society necessarily maintain hypocritical lives. For instance, the millionaire TV anchors who cheer and push the idea of abolishing the police, are themselves guilty of hiring high-security or private police to guard their homes.

On December 22, 2021, US Congresswoman Mary Gay Scanlon (Democrat from Pennsylvania) thanked the "Philadelphia Police Department for their swift response" and efforts to ensure her safety, when she was carjacked earlier that afternoon at gunpoint.[81] Two individuals had approached the congresswoman as she was about to get into her blue 2017 Acura MDX in crime-ridden Philadelphia. The two thugs demanded keys from her and drove away with the car.

Ironically, this same congresswoman had been one of those vocal about defunding the police. In fact, she cosponsored Mental Health Justice Act, which, according to *The Hill*, was intended "to make it easier for state and local governments to defund the police by instead funding mental health services and empowering them to respond to emergency calls instead of armed officers."[82]

Other sponsors of the bill included Representative Ayanna Pressley (Democrat from Massachusetts), Tony Cardenas (Democrat from California),

and Senators Elizabeth Warren (Democrat from Massachusetts), Amy
Klobuchar (Democrat from Minnesota), and Cory Booker (Democrat from
New Jersey).

Even outside the US Congress, such hypocrisy abounds.

Corporate America captains who go on TV to accuse the police of discrimi-
nating against the minority are themselves guilty of not giving a fair share to
those same minorities in their own companies.

The same CEOs of big tech Silicon Valley companies, who consistently
appear on television to decry police discrimination, are often the first ones to
fly to China and India to import a large proportion of their employees from
there. Yet they do not go to Africa, South America, or other parts of the world
to balance their workforce.

The myth that good electrical engineers and computer scientists can only
come from one race in one particular region of the world has no basis today,
in the twenty-first century, when these fields of study are taught in universities all over the world.

The current makeup of Silicon Valley's workforce tells a big story that
should not be ignored. Facebook's workforce comprises 3.8 percent blacks,
5.2 percent Hispanics, and 43 percent Asians.[83] LinkedIn's workforce comprises 3.9 percent blacks, 6 percent Hispanics, and 42 percent Asians.[84]
Apple's workforce comprises 9 percent blacks, 14 percent Hispanics, and 27
percent Asians.[85] Microsoft's workforce comprises 5.7 percent blacks, 7 percent Hispanics, and 35.4 percent Asians.[86] Of course, in all of the companies,
white employees are in the majority.

Since high tech is a high-paying field, the tendency to concentrate hiring
to one race in one part of the world results in a very unequal society. It also
sends a dangerous message to low-level hiring managers about which people
they should hire, given a choice.

Inevitably, it is a consequence of human nature that when human beings of
a particular race or tribe are favored, they immediately assert their superiority.
When Parag Agrawal was appointed as CEO of Twitter, the BBC run a story
commenting on how people of Indian origin, just 1 percent of the US population and 6 percent of the Silicon Valley population, are overrepresented in the
leadership of Silicon Valley.[87]

The article quoted R. Gopalakrishnan as saying, "No other nation in the
world 'trains' so many citizens in such a gladiatorial manner as India does . . .
growing up in India equips Indians to be 'natural managers.'" Incidentally, of
course, Gopalakrishnan did not provide proof to show that other countries do
not train their citizens the same way.

This is where these corporate America bosses demonstrate their hypocrisy.
If they are really concerned about discrimination, and they really think it is
a problem that needs to be solved, why do they have to go to one specific

part of the world to hire a large portion of their workforce while those same educated America minorities remain unemployed and underemployed?

In addition to hypocrisy, political correctness makes the media corrupt and untrustworthy. The inevitable outcome of wanting its reporting to drive certain agendas is that the media has to distort certain facts. It is this distortion of facts that makes the media corrupt and untrustworthy.

A 2020 Gallup/Knight Foundation survey found that the American media is so untrustworthy that more than half of Americans believe that news reporters misrepresent facts, and that inaccuracies in news reporting are purposeful.[88] Consider the following events, where corruption was unmistakable.

On August 25, 2020, a white teenager, Kyle Rittenhouse, fatally shot two men and wounded a third during riots in Kenosha, Wisconsin. The incident occurred amid protests, riots, and civil unrest following the police shooting of a black man in that city. Kyle had gone to the protests with his gun with the intention, as he said, of protecting property. The protests had resulted in looting and destruction of property.

At some point, Rittenhouse was pursued by a group of men. One of them swung a skateboard at him, and another tried to grab his gun. In the process, Rittenhouse fired his gun several times to protect himself. Even though this was a protest against the police killing a black man, all victims of Rittenhouse's shooting were white. There was no indication in his past of any involvement with white supremacists.

Rittenhouse was tried and eventually acquitted on all charges against him. During the trial, the public got to see all evidence the prosecutors had against him. The evidence in court was drastically different from what the media had reported about the incident in the run-up to the trial.

The media twisted, and sometimes just made up, facts.[89] MSNBC contributors branded Rittenhouse as a "domestic terrorist"[90] and the "enemy,"[91] while ABC referred to him as an "alleged white supremacist."[92] None of these characterizations were true. Another prominent journalist decried, in a tweet, the rise of "armed militias, White power groups, Proud Boys, Boogaloo extremists, & Kyle Rittenhouse, a murderer."[93]

For the media, it was important for Rittenhouse to be a white supremacist with extreme hatred for black people. That characterization would fit in perfectly with the media's narrative that black and brown people in America are under siege and in constant fear of being killed by white people. The media was willing to twist facts to achieve this objective.

Another example of media corruption is in the way the media treated students from a catholic high school in Kentucky. On January 8, 2019, a group of students from Covington Catholic High School was in Washington, DC, attending an anti-abortion March for Life.[94] One of the students, Nick Sandmann, was videotaped standing in front of an elderly Native American male who was playing his drum and singing. The elderly Native American, Nathan Phillips, was attending the Indigenous Peoples' March in Washington on the same day.

Sandmann was wearing a MAGA hat. MAGA—Make America Great Again—was a slogan used by candidate Donald Trump during the 2016 presidential campaign. The video of Sandmann standing in front of Phillips went viral and was quickly politicized by the media. The initial narrative by the media was that Sandmann was preventing the elderly man from walking and was also mocking Native American culture. The media went into hysterical mode, attacking and smearing Sandmann and supporters of Donald Trump.

The media was drawn to this story because of its propaganda value. First, here was a white high school kid and supporter of Donald Trump, who appeared to be confronting and disrespecting an elderly Native American. This was politically incorrect. Second, Sandmann and his schoolmates had come to attend an anti-abortion rally. The media is strongly pro-abortion and therefore looks down on such things as anti-abortion rallies.

The media vilified Sandmann as a bigot and racist. All of this character assassination was based on a brief video clip. It later turned out it was the Covington students who were being harassed, and that Sandmann was trying to keep the peace. Sandmann later filed defamation suits against several news outlets. CNN and the *Washington Post* settled out of court.[95]

In their quest to support abortion, the media used distortion and pure corruption to tarnish the names of a group of young innocent anti-abortion marchers. To those who choose to be politically incorrect in defiance of the media, the consequences can be dire.

Consider the following examples of people who lost their careers and their reputations and were even imprisoned for not being politically correct. This is not an attempt to absolve those who use political incorrectness to be mean and hateful. The people on the list were genuinely trying to find solutions to societal problems, but their honesty got them into trouble.

Rick Santorum is an American politician, an attorney by training, and a political commentator. He was the US senator from Pennsylvania from 1995 to 2007. After his tenure in the Senate, Santorum joined CNN as a political commentator. For a long time, he was a lone conservative voice on many panels at CNN. Some of those panels were very large with almost everybody, except Santorum, toeing the liberal line.

Speaking to a group of conservative youth, Santorum pointed out that much of American culture came from Europe. He went on to say, "I mean, yes, we have Native Americans," he said. "But candidly, that—there isn't much Native American culture in American culture."[96]

The condemnation by the media was swift. He was fired from CNN because of those comments. Santorum's point was that religious liberty is important to America because the founding fathers had left Europe to seek religious liberty. They came to America to set up a nation with freedoms they had lacked in Europe. His point was that religious liberty is part of the DNA of America.

Were Santorum's comments not true? While all groups, from Native Americans to African Americans and recent immigrants, have influenced American culture, is it not correct to say that much of the so-called American culture came from Europe?

Nevertheless, Santorum was banished from the mainstream media.

Another high-profile person who tried to fight political correctness is Bill Cosby. Cosby is a comedian, actor, and author. He is also an expert on education, having obtained an EdD (doctorate in education) from the University of Massachusetts, Amherst.

Cosby became very famous for his television show, *The Bill Cosby Show*. The show centered around a model black family in an upper-class neighborhood. It was built on humor and moral messages.[97] Bill Cosby himself was also an activist for black education and excellence.

In his retirement, he was dogged by rumors and accusations of drugging and sexual assault. He always maintained his innocence. After some investigations, Montgomery County district attorney Bruce Castor Jr. declined to criminally prosecute him on February 17, 2005. Whether Cosby was guilty of those crimes or not is an issue the courts may eventually settle, and is certainly beyond the scope of this book.

In any case, by 2014 his legal troubles appeared to be behind him. He was making news for his views on the behavior and values of some poor black people. Starting in 2004, Cosby had railed against what he thought was bad parenting and lack of interest in education among black people.[98] He accused poor black people of "not holding up their end in this deal." [99]

"These people are not parenting. They are buying things for their kids— $500 sneakers for what? And won't spend $200 for 'Hooked on Phonics.' . . . They're standing on the corner, and they can't speak English,"[100] he said.

Bill Cosby had violated an important unwritten rule by placing the blame for black problems on the behavior of some black people, instead of placing it on the white establishment. The media and some corners of the black community were seething with anger; they never forgave him.

On October 16, 2014, Hannibal Buress, a black comedian angry about Cosby's talking down on black people, mocked him by saying, "Pull your pants up, black people . . . I was on TV in the 80s. . . . Yeah, but you rape women, Bill Cosby, so turn the crazy down a couple notches."[101] The video of Buress's performance went viral, and in a short period of time, Bill Cosby's troubles had started piling up again. Tying Cosby's politically incorrect statements to allegations of sexual misconduct did the trick.

As the *Guardian* reported, "Sexual assault allegations had surrounded Cosby for years, but when Buress' stand-up joke went viral, dozens of women came forward."[102]

Adams Serwer of Buzzfeed noted, "Ironically, it was Cosby's decision to hold himself up as a moral exemplar that would bring to light Cosby's admission. . . . A judge unsealed documents in a decade-old lawsuit in part because of Cosby's role as a 'public moralist.'"[103]

Another person who has had to face media repercussions for a politically incorrect opinion is Joanne Rowling. Popularly known by her pen name J. K. Rowling, she is the author of the popular fiction series *Harry Potter*.

J. K. Rowling is a bestselling British author. She was named by *Forbes* as the first billion-dollar author and one of only five self-made female billionaires in the world.[104] In 2014, the Sunday Times's UK Rich List estimated her net worth to be about $1 billion.[105] J. K. Rowling was said to have dropped off the *Forbes* list of billionaires because of her philanthropic giving to several poverty and social-inequality charities. She is estimated to have given away at least $150 million of her fortune.[106]

On May 28, 20202, an opinion piece appeared on Devex, a social enterprise and media platform for the global development community. The article was titled "Opinion: Creating a More Equal Post-COVID-19 World for People Who Menstruate."[107] It was written by three women: Marni Sommer, Virginia Kamowa, and Therese Mahon. The opinion highlighted the extra burden mensuration imposed on women during the coronavirus pandemic:

An estimated 1.8 billion girls, women, and gender non-binary persons menstruate, and this has not stopped because of the pandemic. They still require menstrual materials, safe access to toilets, soap, water, and private spaces in the face of lockdown living conditions that have eliminated privacy for many populations.[108]

The women feared that investment to address "menstrual health and hygiene needs of girls, women, and all people who menstruate" could be reversed because all attention and resources appeared to be focused on the coronavirus.

J. K. Rowling took issue with the title of this opinion piece and tweeted, "'People who menstruate.' I'm sure there used to be a word for those people. Someone help me out. Wumben? Wimpund? Woomud? Opinion: Creating a more equal post-COVID-19 world for people who menstruate."[109]

J. K. Rowling has since faced a lot of criticism and calls for boycotts because of her statements. A UK school dropped her name because of what the school says are her controversial views on transgender issues.[110]

According to the *Washington Post*, US Quidditch and Major League Quidditch "have started the process of changing their names . . . because they want to 'distance' themselves from Rowling 'who has increasingly come under scrutiny for her anti-trans positions in recent years.'"[111] Ironically, the creation of the game of Quidditch in 2005 was inspired by Rowling's *Harry Potter* novels. Even actors who played in many *Harry Potter* adaptations turned against her.[112]

When comedian Dave Chappelle defended J. K. Rowling's comments, he too faced backlash of his own.[113] In comments made in his Netflix special, *The Closer*, Chappelle said, "They canceled J. K. Rowling—my God. Effactually she said gender was a fact, the trans community got mad as s---, they started calling her a trans-exclusionary radical feminist (TERF). I'm team TERF. . . . Gender is a fact."

As the media amasses power to control people, political correctness has become its tool of choice. It is important for the world to fight against this culture of political correctness. The very sustainability of modern civilization depends on it. As the problems of the world become dire, from environmental degradations to energy and water shortages, finding effective solutions to these problems will mean doing away with political correctness.

NOTES

1. Richinick, Michele. "First Lady Michelle Obama: 'Women are smarter than men,'" MSNBC, August 7, 2014, 7:40 AM PDT. https://www.msnbc.com/msnbc /first-lady-michelle-obama-women-are-smarter-men-msna385506; "Mrs. Obama: 'Women are smarter than men,'" CNN Video.

2. Saira, Asher. "Barack Obama: Women are better leaders than men," BBC, December 16, 2019. https://www.bbc.com/news/world-asia-50805822

3. Butterbaugh, Laura, Jackson, April, and Branner, Amy. "Political correctness," *Off Our Backs* 24, no. 8 (1994): 20. http://www.jstor.org/stable/20834894.

4. Purves, Libby. "Political correctness: Who benefits?" *RSA Journal* 147, no. 5489 (1999): 46–53. http://www.jstor.org/stable/41380208

5. Ibid.

6. Ibid.

7. "Gender mainstreaming," Southern Africa Development Community. https:// www.sadc.int/issues/gender/gender-mainstreaming

8. SADC Heads of Government and State. "SADC protocol on gender and development," SADC, August 17, 2008.

9. Friedman, Milton. "The social responsibility of business is to increase its profits," *New York Times* magazine, September 13, 1970.

10. Pishro-Nik, Hossein. *Introduction to Probability Statistics, and Random Processes* (United States: Kappa Research, 2014), 81–105.

11. Jehn, Karen A., Northcraft, Gregory B., and Neale, Margaret A. "Why differences make a difference: A field study of diversity, conflict, and performance in

workgroups," *Administrative Science Quarterly* 44, no. 4 (1999): 741–63. https://doi
.org/10.2307/2667054; Williams, Katherine Y. and O'Reilly, Charles A. "Demography and diversity in organizations: A review of 40 years of research," *Research in
Organizational Behavior* 20 (1998): 77–140.

12. Jehn, Northcraft, and Neale. "Why differences make a difference."

13. Ibid.

14. Ibid.

15. Williams and O'Reilly. "Demography and diversity in organizations."

16. "Women in National Parliaments," Inter-Parliamentary Unit, 2019. http://
archive.ipu.org/wmn-e/classif.htm; "Proportion of seats held by women in national
parliaments (percent)," World Bank. https://data.worldbank.org/indicator/SG.GEN
.PARL.ZS?most_recent_value_desc=true

17. "The most powerful countries in the world," *U.S. News and World Report*, n.d.
https://www.usnews.com/news/best-countries/power-rankings

18. WIPO (2020). World Intellectual Property Indicators 2020. Geneva: World
Intellectual Property Organization.

19. Kopf, Dan. "In one metric of diversity, China comes in dead last," Quartz,
August 15, 2018. https://qz.com/1163632/china-still-has-the-smallest-share-of
-incoming-migrants-in-the-world/

20. Clinton, Hillary Rodham. "Power shortage," *The Atlantic*, October 2020. https:
//www.theatlantic.com/magazine/archive/2020/10/hillary-clinton-womens-rights
/615463/

21. Wong, Tessa. "China angered by Hillary Clinton tweet on women's rights,"
BBC, September 28, 2015. https://www.bbc.com/news/world-asia-china-34377406

22. Dong, Joy. "As Chinese women seek to crack male professions, schools stand
in the way," *New York Times*, November 15, 2021. https://www.nytimes.com/2021/10
/21/world/asia/china-schools-gender-bias.html

23. Wang, Jiayuan. "In the 'three-child' era, China must confront embedded
misogyny," The Diplomat, June 10, 2020. https://thediplomat.com/2021/06/in-the
-three-child-era-china-must-confront-embedded-misogyny

24. Zhao, Jiayi, and Jones, Karen. "Women and leadership in higher education in
China: Discourse and the discursive construction of identity," *Administrative Sciences*
7, no. 3 (2017): 21. https://doi.org/10.3390/admsci7030021

25. Ibid.

26. Ibid.

27. Ibid.

28. Ibid.

29. Ibid.

30. Associated Press and Courtney Kube. "Gen. Mark Milley calls China's hypersonic weapon test 'very concerning,'" NBC News, October 28, 2021, 1:00 AM PDT.
https://www.nbcnews.com/news/world/gen-mark-milley-calls-china-s-hypersonic
-weapon-test-very-n1282606

31. "China has won AI battle with U.S., Pentagon's ex-software chief says,"
Reuters, October 11, 2021, 2:06 PM PDT. https://www.reuters.com/technology/united
-states-has-lost-ai-battle-china-pentagons-ex-software-chief-says-2021-10-11/?

32. Lorenzo, Rocío, Voigt, Nicole, Tsusaka, Miki, Krentz, Matt, and Abouzahr, Katie. "How diverse leadership teams boost innovation," Boston Consultancy Group, January 23, 2018. https://www.bcg.com/en-us/publications/2018/how-diverse -leadership-teams-boost-innovation

33. Lorenzo, Rocio. "How diversity makes teams more innovative," TED Talk, October 2017. https://www.ted.com/talks/rocio_lorenzo_how_diversity_makes _teams_more_innovative#t-278521

34. Ibid.

35. Ibid.

36. Thomas Sowell. *Affirmative Action around the World: An Empirical Study* (New Haven and London: Yale University Press, 2004).

37. Holzer, Harry J., and Neumark, David. "Affirmative action: What do we know?" *Journal of Policy Analysis and Management* 25, no. 2 (Spring 2006): 463–90

38. Ibid.

39. *Missing Pieces Report: The Board Diversity Census of Women and Minorities on Fortune 500 Boards, 6th Edition*, Alliance for Board Diversity (ABD) in collaboration with Deloitte, 2021: https://www2.deloitte.com/content/dam/Deloitte /us/Documents/center-for-board-effectiveness/missing-pieces-fortune-500-board -diversity-study-sixth-edition.pdf

40. Ibid.

41. De Brey, C., Snyder, T. D., Zhang, A., and Dillow, S. A. *Digest of Education Statistics 2019* (NCES 2021–009), National Center for Education Statistics, Institute of Education Sciences, U.S. Department of Education, Washington, DC, 2021. https: //nces.ed.gov/programs/digest/d19/tables/dt19_318.45.asp

42. De Brey, C., Musu, L., McFarland, J., Wilkinson-Flicker, S., Diliberti, M., Zhang, A., Branstetter, C., and Wang, X. (2019). *Status and Trends in the Education of Racial and Ethnic Groups 2018* (NCES 2019–038), National Center for Education Statistics, U.S. Department of Education, Washington, DC, 2019. https://nces.ed.gov /pubsearch/

43. National Center for Education Statistics, Institute of Education Sciences, U.S. Department of Education. https://nces.ed.gov/programs/coe/indicator/coj

44. Gramlich, John. "Black imprisonment rate in the U.S. has fallen by a third since 2006," PEW Research Center, May 6, 2020. https://www.pewresearch.org/fact-tank /2020/05/06/share-of-black-white-hispanic-americans-in-prison-2018-vs-2006/

45. Norton, Leslie P. "The number of Black board members surged after George Floyd's death," *Barron's*, October 27, 2020, 4:41 PM EST. https://www.barrons .com/articles/after-george-floyds-death-the-number-of-black-board-members-surges -51603809011?mod=hp_LEADSUPP_3

46. Willis, Robert J. "A theory of out-of-wedlock childbearing," *Journal of Political Economy* 107, no. S6 (1999): S33–64. https://doi.org/10.1086/250103

47. Keller, Bill. "Mandela and de Klerk square off on TV," *New York Times*, April 15, 1994, A10. https://www.nytimes.com/1994/04/15/world/mandela-and-de-klerk -square-off-on-tv.html; "De Klerk, Mandela pre-election debate rebroadcast, " SABC News, April 14 2019. https://www.youtube.com/watch?v=oTIeqLem67Q

48. "Heart transplant keeps man alive in South Africa; heart transplanted from a dead woman and started by shock is keeping man alive in South Africa," *New York Times*, December 4, 1967, 1. https://www.nytimes.com/1967/12/04/archives/heart-transplant-keeps-man-alive-in-south-africa-heart-transplanted.html

49. Sguazzin, Antony, and Wilson, Leah. "Post-apartheid inequality sparks frustration and fury in South Africa," Bloomberg Businessweek + Equality, August 1, 2021, 9:01 PM PDT. https://www.bloomberg.com/news/articles/2021-08-02/south-africa-dials-back-welfare-as-post-apartheid-inequality-rages

50. "African immigrants in the United States are the nation's most highly educated group," *Journal of Blacks in Higher Education*, no. 26 (1999): 60–61. https://doi.org/10.2307/2999156.

51. Jackson-Obot, Ima. "What makes Nigerians in diaspora so successful," *Financial Times*, October 28, 2020. https://www.ft.com/content/ca39b445-442a-4845-a07c-0f5dae5f3460

52. Gruijters, Rob J., and Behrman, Julia A. "Learning inequality in francophone Africa: School quality and the educational achievement of rich and poor children," *Sociology of Education* 93, no. 3 (July 2020): 256–76. https://doi.org/10.1177/0038040720919379.

53. Heyneman, Stephen P. "A brief note on the relationship between socioeconomic status and test performance among Ugandan primary school children," *Comparative Education Review* 20, no. 1 (1976): 42–47. http://www.jstor.org/stable/1187303.

54. Heyneman, Stephen P. "Why impoverished children do well in Ugandan schools," *Comparative Education* 15, no. 2 (1979): 175–85. http://www.jstor.org/stable/3098481

55. Heyneman, Stephen P., and Loxley, William A. "The effect of primary-school quality on academic achievement across twenty-nine high-and low-income countries," *American Journal of Sociology* 88, no. 6 (1983): 1162–94. http://www.jstor.org/stable/2778968.

56. Kristof, Nicholas. "What's so scary about smart girls?," *New York Times*, May 10, 2014. https://www.nytimes.com/2014/05/11/opinion/sunday/kristof-whats-so-scary-about-smart-girls.html?_r=0

57. Herbert, Paul, Millsap, William, and El, Nagat. "Summative evaluation of USAID/Malawi's girls' attainment in basic literacy and education (GABLE)," The Mitchel Group, Inc./USAID, May 30, 2002. https://pdf.usaid.gov/pdf_docs/Pdabw640.pdf

58. Anzar, Uzma, Harpring, Sharon, Cohen, Joseph and Leu, Elizabeth. "Retrospective pilot study of USAID-funded education projects in Malawi," EQUIP1/USAID, December 2004. https://www.edu-links.org/sites/default/files/media/file/EQUIP1_-_Retrospective_Pilot_Study_of_USAID-funded_Education_Projects_in_Malawi.pdf

59. Ibid.

60. Herbert, Millsap, and El. "Summative evaluation of USAID/Malawi's girls' attainment."

61. Ibid.; Anzar, Harpring, Cohen, and Leu. "Retrospective Pilot Study."

62. Nossiter, Adam. "Nigerian Islamist leader threatens to sell kidnapped girls," *New York Times*, May 5, 2014. https://www.nytimes.com/2014/05/06/world/africa/nigeria-kidnapped-girls.html

63. Ibid.

64. Kristof. "What's so scary about smart girls?"

65. Ibid.

66. Kristof, Nicholas. "'Bring back our girls,'" *New York Times*, May 3, 2014. https://www.nytimes.com/2014/05/04/opinion/sunday/kristof-bring-back-our-girls.html

67. "Michelle Obama's Mother's Day address: A plea for Nigeria's kidnapped girls," ProShare, May 10, 2014. https://www.proshareng.com/news/People/Michelle-Obama-s-Mother-s-Day-Address--A-Plea-for-Nigeria-s-Kidnapped-Girls/23146

68. McKelvey, Tara. "Michelle Obama's hashtag quest to rescue Nigerian girls," BBC News, April 14, 2016. https://www.bbc.com/news/world-us-canada-35948362

69. Ibid.

70. Ibid.

71. House Committee on Foreign Affairs. "Boko Haram: The growing threat to schoolgirls, Nigeria, and beyond," U.S. Government Publishing Office, House Hearing, 113th Congress, May 21, 2014. https://www.govinfo.gov/content/pkg/CHRG-113hhrg88018/html/CHRG-113hhrg88018.htm

72. Rogin, Josh. "Hillary's State Department refused to brand Boko Haram as terrorists," Daily Beast, July 12, 2017. https://www.thedailybeast.com/hillarys-state-department-refused-to-brand-boko-haram-as-terrorists?ref=scroll

73. Roach, Morgan Lorraine. "Boko Haram: Obama fails to designate Nigerian sect a terrorist organization," Heritage Foundation, June 22, 2012. https://www.heritage.org/terrorism/report/boko-haram-obama-fails-designate-nigerian-sect-terrorist-organization

74. Ibid.

75. "Female genital mutilation," UNFPA. https://www.unfpa.org/female-genital-mutilation#readmore-expand

76. Piontek, Elizabeth A, and Albani, Justin M. "Male circumcision: The clinical implications are more than skin deep," *Missouri Medicine* 116, no. 1 (2019): 35–37.

77. Maseko, Nomsa. "When circumcision can mean death in South Africa," Fox News, July 19, 2013. https://www.bbc.com/news/av/world-africa-23378694

78. Meel, B. L. "Traditional male circumcision-related fatalities in the Mthatha area of South Africa," *Medicine, Science, and the Law* 50, no. 4 (2010): 189–91. https://doi.org/10.1258/msl.2010.010017

79. Gonzalez, Laura Lopez. "Over half a million maimed under the knife," Health-E News, June 25, 2014. https://health-e.org.za/2014/06/25/half-million-initiates-maimed-knife/

80. Fogg, Ally. "The death and deformity caused by male circumcision in Africa can't be ignored," *Guardian*, August 25, 2014. https://www.theguardian.com/commentisfree/2014/aug/25/male-circumcision-ceremonies-death-deformity-africa

81. Miller, Andrew Mark. "Democratic congresswoman who sponsored police 'reform' bill carjacked in crime-surging Philadelphia," Fox News, December 22,

2021. https://www.foxnews.com/politics/democratic-congresswoman-defund-police
-carjacked-in-crime-surging-philadelphia

82. Srikanth, Anagha. "New bill funds mental health experts, not police, to respond
to emergencies: 'Mental illness is not a crime,'" *The Hill*, February 26, 2021. https:
//thehill.com/changing-america/well-being/mental-health/540677-new-bill-funds
-mental-health-experts-not-police-to

83. Weinberger, Matt. "Facebook says it wants to 'double our number of women
globally and Black and Hispanic employees in the US' as it reports its annual workforce diversity stats," Business Insider, July 9, 2019, 6.42 PM EST. https://www
.businessinsider.com/facebook-diversity-report-women-workforce-2019-7

84. "Our 2020 workforce diversity report," LinkedIn Corporate Communications,
October 21, 2020. https://news.linkedin.com/2020/october/2020-workforce-diversity
-report

85. "Inclusion & Diversity," Apple, December 2020. https://www.apple.com/
diversity/

86. McIntyre, Lindsay-Rae. "Microsoft's 2021 Diversity & Inclusion report: Demonstrating progress and remaining accountable to our commitments," Official Microsoft Blog, October 20, 2021. https://blogs.microsoft.com/blog/2021/10/20/microsofts
-2021-diversity-inclusion-report-demonstrating-progress-and-remaining-accountable
-to-our-commitments/

87. Inamdar, Nikhil, and Alluri, Aparna. "Parag Agrawal: Why Indian-born CEOs
dominate Silicon Valley," BBC, December 3, 2021. https://www.bbc.com/news/world
-asia-india-59457015?fbclid=IwAR1w9ROuapSDPNxGf_nrOV67fWk4l2aRz1qyW
6UBVfC4ZwovXrG6mmCk7lg

88. "Gallup/Knight Poll: Americans' concerns about media bias deepen, even
as they see it as vital for democracy," Knight Foundation, August 4, 2020. https:
//knightfoundation.org/press/releases/gallup-knight-poll-americans-concerns-about
-media-bias-deepen-even-as-they-see-it-as-vital-for-democracy/

89. Devine, Miranda. "10 heinous lies about Kyle Rittenhouse debunked: Devine,"
New York Post, November 17, 2021, 11:14 PM EST. https://nypost.com/2021/11/17
/10-debunked-heinous-lies-about-kyle-rittenhouse-devine/

90. Kurtz, Howard. "Kyle Rittenhouse, convicted by the media, changes the Kenosha narrative," Fox News, November 12, 2021. https://www.foxnews.com/media/kyle
-rittenhouse-convicted-media-kenosha-narrative-kurtz-media-buzz

91. Morefield, Scott. "MSNBC's Jason Johnson calls Mitch McConnell, Kyle
Rittenhouse 'the enemy,'" Daily Caller, November 4, 2020, 9:01 PM EST. https://
dailycaller.com/2020/11/04/msnbc-jason-johnson-mitch-mcconnell-kyle-rittenhouse
-the-enemy/

92. Prestigiacomo, Amanda. "ABC News calls Kyle Rittenhouse an 'alleged white
supremacist' without evidence, cites Joe Biden," Daily Wire, October 13, 2020.
https://www.dailywire.com/news/abc-news-calls-kyle-rittenhouse-an-alleged-white
-supremacist-without-evidence-cites-joe-biden

93. Ali, Wajahat. Twitter Post, August 29, 2020, 10:17 PM PST. https://twitter.com
/WajahatAli/status/1299939296263245824?s=20

94. London, Matt. "'Covington kid' Nick Sandmann says he's lived under 'constant threat' for over a year," Fox News, April 13, 2020. https://www.foxnews.com/media/nick-sandmann-covington-lincoln-memorial-media

95. Bowden, Ebony. "Washington Post settles $250M suit with Covington teen Nick Sandmann," *New York Post*, July 24, 2020. https://nypost.com/2020/07/24/washington-post-settles-250m-suit-with-covington-teen-nick-sandmann/

96. Stelter, Brian. "Rick Santorum departs CNN after criticism of Native American comments," CNN, May 22, 2021. https://www.cnn.com/2021/05/22/media/rick-santorum-cnn-departure-native-american-criticism/index.html

97. Griffith, Joanne. "The Cosby Show's hidden power," BBC, October 21, 2014. https://www.bbc.com/culture/article/20140919-was-the-cosby-show-revolutionary

98. Lee, Felicia R. "Cosby defends his remarks about poor Blacks' values," *New York Times*, May 22, 2004. https://www.nytimes.com/2004/05/22/arts/cosby-defends-his-remarks-about-poor-blacks-values.html

99. Ibid.

100. Ibid.

101. Francescani, Chris, and Fisher, Luchina. "Timeline of his fall from 'America's Dad' to his release from prison," ABC News, June 20, 2021. https://abcnews.go.com/Entertainment/bill-cosby-trial-complete-timeline-happened-2004/story?id=47799458

102. Graves, Lucia. "Hannibal Buress: How a comedian reignited the Bill Cosby allegations," *The Guardian*, April 26, 2018. https://www.theguardian.com/world/2018/apr/26/hannibal-buress-how-a-comedian-reignited-the-bill-cosby-allegations

103. Serwer, Adam. "Bill Cosby's famous 'pound cake' speech, annotated," BuzzFeed News, July 9, 2015. https://www.buzzfeednews.com/article/adamserwer/bill-cosby-pound-for-pound

104. Watson, Julie, and Kellner, Tomas. "J.K. Rowling and the billion-dollar empire," *Forbes*, February 26, 2004, 3:31 PM EST. https://www.forbes.com/maserati/billionaires2004/cx_jw_0226rowlingbill04.html

105. Giuliano, Karissa, and Whitten, Sarah. "The world's first billionaire author is cashing in," CNBC, August 3, 2015, 11:44 AM EST. https://www.cnbc.com/2015/07/31/the-worlds-first-billionaire-author-is-cashing-in.html; "JK Rowling Net Worth," Celebrity Net Worth. https://www.celebritynetworth.com/richest-celebrities/authors/jk-rowling-net-worth/

106. Ibid.

107. Sommer, Marni, Kamowa, Virginia, and Mahon, Therese. "Opinion: Creating a more equal post-COVID-19 world for people who menstruate," Devex, May 28, 2020. https://www.devex.com/news/sponsored/opinion-creating-a-more-equal-post-covid-19-world-for-people-who-menstruate-97312#.XtwLnv0aEeR.twitter

108. Ibid.

109. Rowling, J.K. Twitter post, June 6, 2020, 2:35 PM PST. https://twitter.com/jk_rowling/status/1269382518362509313?s=20

110. AFP. "UK school drops J.K. Rowling name amid trans row," *Guardian Nigeria*, January 5, 2022. https://guardian.ng/news/uk-school-drops-j-k-rowling-name-amid-trans-row/

111. Beachum, Lateshia. "Real-life quidditch leagues to change Harry Potter sport's name after author's 'anti-trans' remarks," *Washington Post*, December 18, 2021. https://www.washingtonpost.com/arts-entertainment/2021/12/18/quidditch-name/

112. Lenker, Maureen Lee. "Every Harry Potter actor who's spoken out against J.K. Rowling's controversial trans comments," Entertainment, June 10, 2020. https://ew.com/movies/every-harry-potter-actor-whos-spoken-out-against-j-k-rowlings-controversial-transgender-comments/

113. Wong, Wilson. "Dave Chappelle criticized for defending J.K. Rowling in new Netflix comedy special," NBC News, December 6, 2021. https://www.nbcnews.com/news/us-news/dave-chappelle-criticized-defending-j-k-rowling-new-netflix-comedy-n1280928

Chapter 3

How Media Dictatorship Undermines Modern Civilization

On October 13, 2021, a fascinating conversation took place between Joe Rogan and Dr. Sanjay Gupta on Rogan's podcast, the *Joe Rogan Experience*.[1] Their conversation focused on a number of things, but it was the coronavirus discussion that made this conversation interesting.

At the time of the interview, Joe Rogan had just recovered from COVID. His illness was widely publicized because he was one of those who had taken the drug ivermectin to help with COVID recovery.

Dr. Sanjay Gupta is the chief medical correspondent for the CNN. He is probably one of the smartest people in America. On top of being CNN's chief medical correspondent, he is a well-known neurosurgeon who has held faculty positions. He was once nominated for surgeon general but turned it down.[2]

Dr. Gupta would later write that the reason he went on the *Joe Rogan Experience* was to try and reach Rogan's audience, which normally does not watch CNN. He believed that Joe's audience was not well informed about the coronavirus vaccine. As far as he was concerned, CNN did a better job of educating its viewers about the disease.

Dr. Gupta found Rogan to be not exactly as he expected him to be. While concerned about the vaccine and the idea of forcing people to be vaccinated, Rogan was actually not against the coronavirus vaccine. The interview became more memorable when Rogan asked Dr. Gupta why CNN, as he put it, "lied" that he (Rogan) had taken a horse dewormer drug as medicine for coronavirus.

"Don't you think that a lie like that is dangerous on a news network when you know that they know they're lying? . . . Do you think that that's a problem that your news network lies?," Rogan asked. To support his point, he played a clip of the CNN *OutFront* show in which host Erin Burnett reported that Rogan had taken a "drug used for livestock."

It is important to understand that the Rogan-Gupta interview took place to a background of a politically charged atmosphere. The coronavirus pandemic, which hit America during the 2020 presidential election, had been highly politicized. Americans were very divided in their views on both the coronavirus and its vaccine.

Conservatives largely viewed official government statements on the pandemic with a lot of skepticism. Quite a significant number of conservatives and others did not even trust the vaccine. In fact, as of November 2021, a third of all Americans had chosen not to be vaccinated yet.[3] The media had used this vaccine hesitance to brand conservatives as having backward or unintelligent views.

And so when Erin Burnett claimed that the conservative Joe Rogan had taken "medicine for livestock," she was really tapping into this liberal partisan talking point. This is why Rogan pushed back hard on Dr. Gupta during their chat. Dr. Gupta appeared very uncomfortable with this part of their conversation. He, however, conceded that it was wrong for CNN to call ivermectin horse dewormer medicine. He said he did not know why any anchor on his network would refer to the medicine as a livestock drug.

To which Rogan replied, "You didn't ask, you are the medical guy there?"

It is not clear whether Rogan knew the significance of this question when he posed it. Yet this is a very important question because it encapsulates the signs of our times. Why would Dr. Gupta, a highly qualified medical doctor, in charge of medical analysis on a major news network, stand aside helplessly as the network he represents disseminates apparent erroneous medical facts?

The media establishment has become so powerful that even brilliant experts, like Dr. Gupta, have to bow down to it. The media can disseminate any information it wants, and experts must either endorse it or be in danger of losing their jobs. The result is a disturbing trend where experts, because they have to tailor their analysis to the desire of the media, are increasingly getting predictions wrong.

These have not been the best of times for experts in America. The experts who frequented the television to convince the public that Iraq had weapons of mass destruction were wrong. After a long costly war, it was found that Iraq did not have weapons of mass destruction.

The Trump-Russia collusion sandal that dominated the airwaves for much of Donald Trump's presidency ended up being a hoax. The media embellished the claim possibly because they did not want Trump as their president. The legal experts who swore that the Trump-Russia collusion would be established with facts were wrong.

Predictions of a landslide victory for candidate Hillary Clinton in the 2016 presidential elections ended with a huge disappointment for Clinton supporters. Among those many supporters were members of the media themselves.

Common to all of these wrong predictions is the fact that the predictions erred in the direction of what the media at the time had hoped the outcome would be. In other words, the power of the media intimidated or influenced the experts to make those erroneous predictions.

Experts are under pressure to endorse the networks or lose their jobs. It is not uncommon to see one expert say other thing on one news network but lean in another direction when appearing on another network with a different ideology.

Sometimes the media simply uses naïve experts to advance its own messages. Consider how the media used Dr. Anthony Fauci during the coronavirus pandemic. Dr. Fauci is the director of the National Institute of Allergy and Infectious Diseases (NIAID) and the chief medical advisor to the US president. He has been a scientist at the NIAID for some time. He is also the person in charge of coordinating the fight against the coronavirus in America.

To the media, the coronavirus pandemic provided a way to do away with President Trump, whom they disliked very much. His election to the presidency in 2016 had been a surprise and shock to the media. The media would now make sure that they get rid of him in the 2020 elections. There was now an opportunity to use the pandemic as an albatross around Trump's neck in a presidential election year.

The narrative the media created was that things could have gotten better quickly if Trump had done certain things faster or better. When the number of coronavirus deaths reached two hundred thousand on September 22, 2020, CNN almost blamed Trump for the deaths.[4] The assumption was that another president could have avoided those deaths.

The media sought to portray Dr. Fauci as an all-intelligent, infallible expert whose views were in direct conflict with President Trump's views. Anybody who disagreed or questioned Dr. Fauci was described as anti-science. Dr. Fauci appeared in the press regularly to talk about coronavirus. He became a very well-known figure. No other name in America was more associated with the 2020 coronavirus pandemic than that of Anthony Fauci.

He made pronouncements on the disease with so much more certainty than perhaps any good scientist should on an emerging scientific problem. Scientists always give room for the possibility that their views could change given more information. Yet, at every point, Dr. Fauci spoke as if he was giving an unchanging gospel truth.

Dr. Fauci's image as an infallible medical genius was difficult to sustain because, while he spoke with authority, he also seemed to change his statements quite often. For instance, as news reports of the pandemic emerging in China reached America, Dr. Fauci urged people to be calm, and assured Americans that they have more to fear from seasonal flu than coronavirus.[5] Obviously, this advice had to be changed very quickly.

Dr. Fauci also initially advised against masks saying, "There's no reason to be walking around with a mask. When you're in the middle of an outbreak, wearing a mask might make people feel a little bit better and it might even block a droplet, but it's not providing the perfect protection that people think that it is. And, often, there are unintended consequences—people keep fiddling with the mask and they keep touching their face."[6]

Later on, however, he went against his own advice and started putting on a mask, himself. In fact, at one point, he appeared before Congress wearing three masks at the same time.[7] Of course, it is normal for scientists to change or modify their views, especially on a fast-emerging phenomenon such as the coronavirus infections. However, the problem with Dr. Fauci was that sometimes when he had to change statements, he did so in a less than candid manner.

When he initially discouraged the public from walking around with masks, he specifically pointed out that masks gave people a false sense of protection and encouraged people to touch their faces.[8] Yet, when his advice changed, he insisted that he had earlier on only discouraged people from wearing masks because he did not want first responders to feel the strain of a shortage of personal protection equipment.[9] This lack of clarity added to more public mistrust. He gave the impression of giving a political answer to a scientific question. People expect their scientists to always tell the public the truth regardless of the politics.

Dr. Fauci was not particularly media savvy and played right into the hands of a media that had its own agenda. His love of appearing on television proved a liability as he became vulnerable to such vanities as praise from the media. The media lavished praised on him, especially when he seemed to go against his boss, Donald Trump. The media loved him so much that he found himself on covers of prestigious magazines of fashion and style.[10]

In the end, Dr. Fauci was seen as partisan by a significant fraction of Americans. He was blamed for politicizing the pandemic.[11] Perhaps Dr. Fauci's greatest mistake was that he did not discourage the press from attacking those who questioned him. He himself famously characterized attacks on him as "quite frankly . . . attacks on science."[12] In doing so, he indirectly enabled and encouraged an atmosphere of fear and censorship in which anybody who questioned his ideas was regarded as anti-science and dangerous. At this point, the media had him where they wanted him to be.

In this atmosphere of fear and censorship, high-tech social media started censoring any views or scientists that questioned Dr. Fauci or government official statements on the coronavirus. Facebook, Twitter, and Google started either labeling or removing information they thought was misleading to the general public on the coronavirus. And it so happened that most of the views happened to be those by conservatives and Republicans.

This disturbing culture of censorship did not spare scientific literature. On February 19, 2020, a group of scientists signed and published a letter in the medical journal *Lancet*.[13] The letter praised Chinese scientists for "transparent sharing of data" and condemned anybody who wanted investigations into the origins of the coronavirus. This letter came within three months of the advent of coronavirus pandemic. Certainly not enough time to draw definite conclusions and shut down debates on an emerging pandemic.

The same authors followed this first letter with another one eighteen months later, on July 5, 2021.[14] The new letter was a bit toned down and called for scientists to work together to find out how SARS-CoV-2 reached the human population. However, they still insisted that "the strongest clue from new, credible, and peer-reviewed evidence in the scientific literature is that the virus evolved in nature, while suggestions of a laboratory-leak source of the pandemic remain without scientifically validated evidence that directly supports it in peer-reviewed scientific journals."

As Jacques van Helden and his colleagues pointed out in their own communication, the statement by these scientists had a "silencing effect on the wider scientific debate, including among science journalists."[15] Van Helden and his colleagues even noted that the scientists' arguments were not factual. In fact, "There is no direct support for the natural origin of SARS-CoV-2, and a laboratory-related accident is plausible," Van Helden and his colleagues stated.

The politicization of scientific publication did not stop there. Even the respected journal *Nature* ran an article in which it claimed that, during the Trump administration, scientists were sidelined, silenced, and ignored.[16] This despite the fact that Dr. Fauci would be allowed to disagree with the president, even while sharing the same podium at a press conference, with no consequences at all.[17] Most of the other scientists, either from the government or the private sector, were always on television sharing their views all the time.

The media establishment also became obsessed with refuting off-the-cuff medical statements made by the former president, who is not even a doctor. The obsession was so much that even professionals put forward half-baked research just to prove that the president was wrong.

In White House weekend briefings on April 4 and 5, 2020, President Trump touted possible therapeutic properties of hydroxychloroquine against the coronavirus. As Dr. Fauci rightly pointed out at the same press conference, there was no scientific evidence to support the use of hydroxychloroquine on coronavirus patients. The media, however, blew this out of proportion. It paraded television experts from all over to refute the idea that hydroxychloroquine could have been therapeutic.

The eagerness to prove that the president wrong was so much that some scientists even presented articles for publication with fabricated or nonexistent data. One such article appeared in the prestigious medical journal *Lancet* on May 22, 2020. The article claimed to show the lack of "benefit of hydroxychloroquine or chloroquine, when used alone or with a macrolide, on in-hospital outcomes for COVID-19."[18]

This article was quickly cited in the mainstream media. Yet it did not take long before the article was retracted by the journal. The authors said they could no longer vouch for the veracity of the primary data sources. The media had hijacked the coronavirus messaging for its own purpose of getting rid of Donald Trump. The reporting on the coronavirus was centered, not around the telling of the truth but, rather, on the elimination of the Trump presidency. Thus, everything the incumbent administration, especially the president, said had to be fought against.

The media religiously combed Dr. Fauci's statements for any apparent disagreement with Trump. Even when Trump suggested at a press confer-ence that a solution to coronavirus infections could involve using something with coronavirus-killing properties such as detergent, the media quickly pounced on it and accused him of advising Americans to inject themselves with detergent.

Even though this was on national television, the major news networks shamelessly reported the distortion with impunity. CNN ran an article titled "Fact Check: Trump Dangerously Suggests Sunlight and Ingesting Disinfectants Could Help Cure Coronavirus."[19] The media also used other scientists for its own political gains, and misdirected scientific thought. For example, the coronavirus models, developed by scientists, were twisted or taken out of context to prove that Trump was at fault for the fast propagation of the disease in America.

Early coronavirus models were unreliable largely because this was a new virus. Some of the models used, such as the University of Washington's Institute for Health Metrics and Evaluation (IHME), were simplistic and could not be relied upon beyond a short period of time. Not only did the IHME model fail to make good future predictions, but it also wrongly assumed that social-distancing measures, once put in place, were always suf-ficient to rapidly decrease case numbers to zero.[20]

For the media, however, the IHME predictions were gospel truth. When the model underpredicted actual numbers, the media would blame Donald Trump for what the media believed was his inability to implement strict anti-coronavirus measures quickly and property. In the media's thinking, the model predictions had to be correct and would have matched with the actual numbers only if government had done its due diligence.

The truth is that the scientific intention of building such models is not to give accurate predictions, but simply to provide a rough guide for making decisions. Even at their best, models like the IHME cannot be relied upon to give predictions beyond just a few days, especially when it is difficult to get accurate actual numbers of infected people. Even the more sophisticated models would still suffer from the fact that the pathways through which coronavirus was spread from one person to another were not well understood.[21]

Initial model projections of a previously unknown pandemic are almost always never going to be exact. Yet, as was seen in the early days of the coronavirus pandemic, those initial modeling efforts are likely to be vulnerable to political manipulations. Briggs and Littlejohn warn that "it is incumbent upon guardians of the public trust in health-care institutions and services to remain apolitical—to remain focused on scientific knowledge and the needs of public health."[22]

The pettiness of the anti-Trump sentiments reached a maximum when veteran journalist and author Bob Woodward accused Trump of having known the devastating nature of the pandemic as early as February 2020. The media jumped on this story and, once again, accused Trump of being responsible for the deaths of thousands of Americans.

The media chose not to check the basic facts or ask serious questions about this claim. Keep in mind that this was a virus that was new. Even experts in China did not completely understand the nature of the disease. A simple review of the disease timeline will show how ridiculous this claim was.

Around the same time, on January 14, 2020, the World Health Organization (WHO) had tweeted that preliminary investigations by Chinese authorities had found no clear evidence of human-to-human transmission of the coronavirus.[23]

On January 22 and 23, 2020, the WHO director convened an emergency committee under the International Health Regulations to assess whether COVID-19 outbreak constituted a public health emergency of international concern.[24] That committee, consisting of independent, international experts, was unable to reach a consensus based on the evidence available at the time.

As noted earlier, about the same time, even Dr. Fauci did not think the coronavirus was a bigger risk than seasonal flu. In an interview on February 15, 2020, Dr. Fauci pointed out that not much was not known about coronavirus. And just as Trump said elsewhere, Fauci agreed that it was reasonable to assume that the coronavirus would be seasonal.[25] So how could Trump have been certain as to how the virus would devastate America at a time when all of these experts, including Dr. Fauci, the WHO, and Chinese scientists did not know much about the virus?

Bob Woodward's allegation was not the first media attempt to tie the coronavirus as an albatross around Trump's neck. In April 2021, ABC News reported that the National Center for Medical Intelligence (NCMI) had warned the president in late 2019 that the novel disease in China would pose a major threat to US forces in the region, and eventually devastate the United

States.[26] The report sought to place blame on the administration in that, based on that report, the administration "could have ramped up mitigation and containment efforts far earlier to prepare for a crisis."[27]

The ABC News report galvanized the media as they stood united in their condemnation of the administration. Very little effort was spent in finding out whether the report was true or false. By the end of the day, however, the director of the NCMI issued a rare denial,[28] saying while his agency's practice is not to comment publicly on specific intelligence matters, because of the need for transparency in an unprecedented pandemic, they were forced to confirm that the news report was false. No such NCMI product had existed.

Nobody had, or could have, secret information on how the coronavirus would eventually affect the globe. The waves of the pandemic and the variants that came up during the period could not have been predicted by any scientific models.

All available information on the virus was already in the public. As the vice chairman of the Joint Chiefs of Staffs, John Hyten, said at the time, the first indications the administration had were "the reports out of China in late December that were in the public forum. And the first intel reports were in January."[29]

The truth is that astute observers looking at news from China could only speculate what would happen in America. Fox News host Tucker Carlson had warned about a possible pandemic coming out of China simply by looking at news reports from China. In January 2020, Carlson said on his program:

> Well, consider the stories they're downplaying in favor of a protracted government hearing whose ending we already know. For starters, at this very moment, a serious viral outbreak is spreading across China, the world's biggest country. In just a matter of weeks, this new strain of coronavirus has generated almost as many new cases as SARS did. Remember SARS?[30]

The media at the time overlooked the stories from China and instead concentrated on first rooting for Trump impeachment hearings and then covering the hearings wall to wall.

In 2019 the Democratic-led House of Representatives impeached then President Donald Trump on his dealings with Ukraine and his handling of congressional subpoenas. According to protocol, the president was then tried before the Senate. The result was a foregone conclusion in that the Senate was controlled by Republicans, who overwhelmingly did not believe that the president should have been removed from office.

The media, being overwhelmingly in support of the impeachment, gave the trials wall-to-wall coverage. The Senate trials were held around January/February 2020, at the time when the coronavirus was raging in China.

Ironically during this time, it was the media that played down the impending pandemic. Consider the following headlines from some of the major news networks in the country.

On January 29, 2020, the *Los Angeles Times* published an op-ed titled "The New Coronavirus Isn't a Threat to People in the United States—but Flu Is."[31] The editorial described public initiatives to wear masks as overkill because they "signal that we should be deathly afraid of something that does not currently pose a threat and may well never do so." The op-ed went on to quote Dr. Fauci, who had told the op-ed writer, "I think we can say right now, given what's going on, that the risk to the American public is low. But that doesn't mean they shouldn't be taking this situation very seriously, which is what we as health authorities are doing."

On the same day, January 29, 2020, *Wired* demanded that, "We Should Deescalate the War on the Coronavirus."[32] The publication decried what it described as "Fear, finger-pointing, and militaristic action against the virus are unproductive" instead of just adjusting to a new normal of periodic outbreaks.

KQED run a story tilted, "The Flu Is Still a Bigger Health Threat in the U.S. than Novel Coronavirus."[33] While the article acknowledged the devastating effect of the coronavirus in China, it still insisted, "In the U.S., the real threat to my health and yours is this year's flu."

CNN was much more concerned about what it called racism and xenophobia. On January 31, the news network posted on its website an article titled "As the Coronavirus Spreads, Fear Is Fueling Racism and Xenophobia."[34] The article was worried about the panic about the coronavirus that appeared to have taken "more familiar form, with the re-emergence of old racist tropes that portray Asians, their food, and their customs as unsafe and unwelcome."

Time's headline for January 31, 2020, was, "Want to Protect Yourself From Coronavirus? Do the Same Things You Do Every Winter."[35] The magazine equated coronavirus prevention measures to those used against seasonal flu.

"Many Americans likely grew a little nervous after the U.S. Centers for Disease Control and Prevention (CDC) announced Thursday that a novel coronavirus has spread for the first time within the U.S. But agency officials and other doctors have a simple message for Americans: keep doing what you're doing to stay healthy," the magazine said.

On February 1, 2020, the *Washington Post* had the headline "Get a Grippe, America. The Flu Is a Much Bigger Threat than Coronavirus, for Now."[36] The article said, "Clearly, the flu poses the bigger and more pressing peril; a handful of cases of the new respiratory illness have been reported in the United States, none of them fatal or apparently even life-threatening."

USA Today's headline on the same day was "Coronavirus Is Scary, but the Flu Is Deadlier, More Widespread."[37] While acknowledging the presence of coronavirus, the article said that influenza was "something more dangerous and much deadlier" that had been infecting millions of Americans.

"Why are we panicked about coronavirus—and calm about the flu?" the *Hill* asked on February 4, 2020. The paper said, "Although the flu has killed 10,000 Americans already this season and no Americans have died of the coronavirus, there's a psychological reason we fear the new virus more."[38] It is because human beings are wired to fear unknowns more than the evils they know, the paper argued.

The *Daily Beast* complained, "The Virus Killing U.S. Kids Isn't the One Dominating the Headlines."[39] The paper wondered why the headlines were about coronavirus, which had no fatality at the time, while the flu, with dozens of deaths, was not in the headlines. The paper noted that even after flu deaths, there was not public panic, no mass buying of face masks as had happened for the then new coronavirus.

Even as late as February 13, 2020, a WICS/WRSP headline still insisted, "Experts Warn Flu Is Greater Risk than Coronavirus."[40] It said, "New information about the spread of the novel coronavirus continues to come out. While many are worried about contracting the virus, experts say you should worry about something else . . . flu continues to pose a much greater risk to people in central Illinois and the rest of the United States."

The Associated Press, on February 18, 2020, erroneously emphasized that the flu is more deadly than coronavirus. "Is the New Virus More 'Deadly' than Flu? Not Exactly,"[41] their headline said. Even at the end of February, the AZ Central's headline was that the "New Coronavirus Is Likely to Go Pandemic, but That's No Reason to Panic or Overreact."[42] The article described coronavirus as easy to spread but not as lethal as the flu.

The way the media conducted itself during the 2020 pandemic is a classic example of how dangerous the rise of media power is to freedom of thought, science, and democracy. As government struggled to respond to the novel virus, the media's eye was on the 2020 presidential elections.

Another instance in which media power led to a disastrous consequence for society was the botched predictions for the outcome of the 2016 presidential elections. Before the elections, the media and its pundits were just too sure that Hillary Clinton would win the elections. The 2016 presidential elections pitted a politically incorrect Republican candidate, Donald Trump, and a liberal media favorite, Hillary Clinton.

After Barack Obama won his second term, it was highly anticipated that Hillary Clinton would represent the Democratic Party at the next elections. The media loved Clinton and wanted to do everything to help her. After all, she would be the first woman president of the United States.

About the same time, there was a major change in the media landscape. Jeff Zucker was appointed to take over at CNN as its CEO. Zucker would go on to change CNN from being almost the only truly centrist news network to a leftist news organization.[43] Prior to this, CNN had truly been a trusted news organization where most people would turn to for any breaking news.

One of the first things Zucker did at CNN was to put plans in process to produce a Hillary Clinton movie. This was a controversial move and, at the same time, a strong signal that CNN would be supporting Hillary Clinton in the upcoming 2016 election. Although Allison Gollust, the CNN senior vice president of communications, insisted that the network's editorial staff would have no role in the production of the movie, the decision was a major departure from CNN's known culture and philosophy.

As Politico noted at the time, "The film adds yet another installment to the growing list of Hillary-related television projects and books slated for release before the 2016 presidential campaign. But it also presents a potential image problem for CNN's News division as it covers Clinton in the run-up to her highly anticipated bid for the White House.[44]"

Another major news network, NBC, announced in July 2013 plans to produce a Hillary Clinton miniseries. The setting of the miniseries would be from 1998, at about the time when the Clinton family was engulfed in the Monica Lewinsky sex scandal. This was a sure way to drum up sympathy for possible candidate Hillary Clinton in the run-up to the 2016 presidential elections. Gary Leven of *USA Today* described the proposed miniseries as "sure-to-be-controversial,"[45] given that Hillary Clinton was widely expected to make a second presidential run in 2016.

Both CNN and NBC scrapped their plans for the Hillary Clinton productions when the Republican Party threatened to exclude the networks from holding presidential debates.[46] The Republican committee chair said CNN and NBC had shown "clear favoritism" and would not be hosting a single Republican primary debate if they did not drop their plans.[47]

Nevertheless, the stage was set for what would be one of the most biased election coverages in history. In the run-up to the election, the media strongly favored Clinton. All the analysis on television only highlighted Clinton's chances. Any other contrary evidence was ignored.

Writing in the *New York Post* a few months before the 2016 elections, Salena Zito described the difference between the mood on the ground and what media pundits were predicting on television. She wrote:

If you drive anywhere in Pennsylvania, from the turnpike to the old US routes to the dirt roads connecting small towns like Hooversville with "bigger" small towns like Somerset, you might conclude that Donald Trump is ahead in this state by double digits. Large signs, small signs, homemade signs, signs that wrap around barns, signs that go from one end of a fence to another dot the landscape with such frequency that, if you were playing the old-fashioned road-trip game of counting cows, you would hit 100 in just one small town like this one.

In Ruffsdale, I am pretty sure I saw more than 100 Trump signs. It's as if people here have not turned on the television to hear pundits drone on and on about how badly Trump is losing in Pennsylvania. It's not just visual: In interview after interview in all corners of the state, I've found that Trump's support across the ideological spectrum remains strong. Democrats, Republicans, independents, people who have not voted in presidential elections for years—they have not wavered in their support.[48]

After the historic election, *Washington Post* correspondent Philip Bump blamed himself for not foreseeing the Trump victory as he should have. Bump recalled how on November 5, 2016, he had visited both the Clinton and Trump campaign headquarters around Scranton, Pennsylvania.

Bump had found an almost deserted Clinton campaign headquarters, in stark contrast to the vibrant Trump campaign headquarters, a distance away, a bit outside of town. The Trump campaign headquarters appeared to have energized people, some working the phones and others coming to visit from far away. Bump was surprised by the energy in the Trump campaign, given how much was written about Trump's inattention to the ground game. After the elections, Bump wrote:

I can look at that moment as significant and revelatory: How'd I miss Trump's win, having seen what I saw in Scranton? A few days before, I'd even written a story pointing out that Trump was closer to the presidency than he'd been at any other point in the campaign. A few days before that, I'd noted that undecideds appeared to be breaking to Trump, boosting him in the polls. But going into Election Day, I still expected Hillary Clinton to win.[49]

On the morning of November 9, 2016, the morning after the election, Joe Scarborough on his morning show described the election as a "complete earthquake." He then attacked the media's role saying, "The media was all in on this narrative, and everybody was marching in lockstep . . . Clinton is going to win! Clinton is going to win!"[50]

But it was his colleague, MSNBC contributor Mike Barnicle, who summarized the whole election properly when he said:

It was just people who were going to vote for Donald Trump no matter what. No matter what he said, no matter what he did, and how he behaved. They were determined to vote for Donald Trump, and they were ignored. They were ignored by pollsters. They were ignored by the media. And they showed up yesterday in astounding numbers, a wave of people across the country.[51]

There was no question that media wanted Hillary Clinton to win the 2016 election, and they tailored their coverage to a Hillary Clinton landslide victory. A review of Twitter archives shows a media that was strongly pro-Clinton, that was excited before the night of November 8, 2016, and very sad and frustrated after the night of November 8, 2016. The excitement was due to the anticipated win for Clinton, and the frustration and sadness was a reaction to the Trump win.

The story of the 2016 election and all recent presidential elections in America, generally, is a story of a media landscape consistently trying to force their candidate on the people. The election coverage was so one-sided that if such elections were held in Zimbabwe or Russia, America would have rejected the election on the basis that the electorate was not fully informed properly.

In fact, it is surprising that in spite of all the media's biased coverage, Trump still went ahead and won. One wonders how much bigger the victory would have been if the coverage was balanced. Biased election coverage is a form of propaganda or even gaslighting. In the 2016 elections, every effort was made by the media to paint a picture of a Hillary win. Eccentric "experts" who would normally have gotten pushback in a free and fair press were given free rein as long as they predicted a win for Hillary Clinton.

A Princeton University professor was so certain of his prediction for a Hillary Clinton win that he promised to eat a bug if Donald Trump were to win.[52] "It is totally over," the professor tweeted. "If Trump wins more than 240 electoral votes, I will eat a bug." The tweet has since been deleted. As it turned out, he indeed ended up eating the bug on live television.

After the elections, the media and its pundits tried to explain their botched predictions by claiming that the polls were wrong. Nothing could be further from the truth. Polling guru, Nate Silver pointed out that the bad predictions were due to confirmation bias coupled with good old-fashioned liberal media bias:

> Journalists just didn't believe that someone like Trump could become president, running a populist and at times also nationalist, racist and misogynistic campaign in a country that had twice elected Obama and whose demographics supposedly favored Democrats. So, they cherry-picked their way through the data to support their belief, ignoring evidence—such as Clinton's poor standing in the Midwest—that didn't fit the narrative.[53]

Silver believed that even though most of the polls in swing states showed Clinton in the lead, those leads were within the margin of error and had been shrinking in the last few days of the campaign. The idea that everybody thought Clinton was sure to win reflected elite groupthink, "and it came despite the polls as much as because of the polls."[54]

Silver believes that there is such a thing as a liberal media bubble. In 2013, less than 10 percent of journalists identified as Republicans. Only 3 percent of the major newspapers endorsed Trump, while Clinton got the rest.[55] As Curt Anderson put it, "Most of the press and folks in DC were science deniers when it came to this election . . . Even in the face of polls that showed it very close, they all said that Trump had almost no chance. It was because they couldn't imagine it happening. . . . They are in a bubble, and that bubble has just been burst."[56]

The 2016 election coverage in America shows an example of how a powerful media can engineer an election toward its own preferred candidates, thereby robbing power from citizens. This is an example of how harmful a media with oversized power can be to our democracy. Yes the media failed to swing the 2016 election. But then it is impossible to know how many other times it succeeded in swinging by creating false narratives. Joe Biden won the 2020 presidential elections while doing minimal campaign events or television appearances. Could he have won that election if the media had not campaigned for him and against Donald Trump?

Another area where media influence can have bad consequences for society is the area of climate change. In the twenty-first century, nothing brings passion out of the general public more than issues of climate change and global warming. Yet no phenomenon is more complex and expensive to model and predict than climate change.

Coronavirus modeling, with all its wrong models, overestimations, and underestimations, is peanuts compared to climate change. With coronavirus, scientists could test their models in a matter of weeks and know whether the modeling was correct or not. Their mechanistic models could mimic the way SARS-CoV-2 spreads as much as possible since there are few parameters involved, and most of the pathways for the spread of the disease are known.

Climate change modeling, on the other hand, involves a lot of parameters interacting in a complex manner. It also takes a long time to verify whether models that explain data well can also predict the future properly. Current models of climate change show the Earth warming with humans being responsible for it. We should trust science for it represents our best knowledge on any subject. Yet it is also important to remember that scientists work with the best knowledge they have at that particular point in time. Nonscientists have a hard time understanding this. And this where it becomes dangerous when the media gets involved in scientific debates.

On November 11, 2013, a fascinating debate took place on *Piers Morgan Live* on CNN. Host Piers Morgan had asked Roy Spencer and Mark

Hertsgaard to debate whether the devastating typhoon that had just hit the Philippines was partly caused by climate change.

Dr. Roy Spencer received his BS in atmospheric sciences from the University of Michigan in 1978, and his MS and PhD in meteorology from the University of Wisconsin in 1980 and 1982. He is a principal research scientist at the University of Alabama in Huntsville, and the US Science Team leader for the Advanced Microwave Scanning Radiometer on NASA's Aqua satellite.[57] Mark Hertsgaard is a journalist. He is the executive director and cofounder of Covering Climate Now. According to Wikipedia, Hertsgaard received a BA in international studies from Johns Hopkins University in 1977.[58]

Dr. Spencer started the debate by saying, "The earth is a little warmer right now. We're not exactly sure whether it's 100 percent due to mankind, or 50 percent due to mankind, 50 percent due to nature and by chance."[59]

In reply, Hertsgaard says with passion, "Dr. Spencer, that is not true, sir. That is not true. You are misstating the facts . . . To say that we don't know? Listen to what the IPCC [Intergovernmental Panel on Climate Change] just said in its report: 'That humankinds' activities are now responsible for most of this.' Frankly, I don't know why, Dr. Spencer, I believe that you don't even agree that climate change is man-made, last time I checked. If you've revised your position, I'd love to hear about it. To listen to you talk about climate change, that man-made climate change you reject that 99 . . . so you stand against the 97 percent of scientists who say this?"[60]

One of these gentlemen was a scientist (Dr. Spencer) and the other a journalist (Hertsgaard). The debate showed the disconnect between scientists and nonscientists, and why essentially it is dangerous to have the media lead a scientific debate. First, Hertsgaard's only argument in the debate appears to be, "this is true because 97% of scientists say so." The argument is in itself unscientific. In many scientific debates, scientific papers, and countless numbers of scientific journals, scientists hardly ever use the argument that some concept is true because 99 percent of scientists believe it.

They do not use it because if it was a good argument, then Galileo Galilei's position would not have prevailed. Galileo Galilei lived from 1564 to 1642 AD. He was the scientist who famously stood for the correct theory that the Earth rotates on its axis and revolves around the sun once every year. The Church at the time, and all other scientists, believed that it was the sun that revolved around the Earth. His thoughts were considered heretical, in contradiction to the Bible, and he was imprisoned for that.

Science is decided by facts, not democracy.

Second, Hertsgaard's performance demonstrates one of the challenges science faces in the twenty-first century. Science has become too successful for its own good. It now affects our lives from technological advancements to wonderful cures and nutrition. Science has become an "in thing" so much that everybody wants to speak on scientific issues with authority, even if they have not been trained in science. Yet it takes many years of rigorous scientific training for anybody to be a scientist or science expert. It is impossible for a nonscientist to speak with authority on science. Nonscientists do not think in the same way as scientists do, and thus these two groups do not function the same way.

In a book titled *The Unnatural Nature of Science: Why Science Does Not Make Sense*,[61] Lewis Wolpert argues that scientists use scientific sense to analyze the world, whereas the general public uses common sense. Wolpert notes that common sense is not a trivial thing: "It reflects an enormous amount of information that one has gained about the world and provides a large number of practical rules—many of them quite logical—for dealing with day-to-day life."[62]

Science, on the other hand tries to explain nature at a fundamental level. It uses rigorous theories to explain natural phenomena. Such theories must be capable of being tested to both confirm and falsify them. The theories must also leave room to be improved upon or abandoned when evidence demands it. Scientific ideas cannot be obtained by simple inspection of phenomena.[63]

For example, common sense will tell a person that the Earth is flat. That observation fits in with natural expectation. All the five senses testify to a flat Earth. A careful nonscientific analysis of whether the Earth is round or flat will make a person conclude that the Earth is flat. These days, when most nonscientists are asked whether the Earth is round or flat, they will quickly say that the Earth is round. They say that, not because they used their own analysis to arrive at the conclusion, but rather because they heard scientists say it. But if asked whether they can offer proof that the Earth is indeed round, a vast majority of these nonscientists will not.

It actually takes scientific reasoning to conclude that the Earth is round. It turns out that it is not that simple to come to that conclusion. According to a NASA website,[64] it is believed that scientists have known that the Earth is round since the time of the ancient Greeks. Pythagoras proposed that the Earth was round nearly 2,500 years ago. He might have based his reasoning by observing the shape of a partial moon as the moon moved through its orbital cycle. He reasoned that if the moon was round then the Earth must be round, too.[65]

Anaxagoras concluded and agreed that the Earth was round based on the shape of the Earth's shadow on the Moon during a lunar eclipse.[66] And finally, Aristotle concluded that the Earth was round based on constellations one could see in the sky as one moves further and further from the equator.[67] The proof that the Earth is round is not so simple, is it?

As complicated as it sounds, this is how scientists are trained to approach problems in nature. Common sense does not require such rigorous analysis of phenomena. If the summers get cooler two years in a row, the public is more likely to believe that the Earth is getting colder, and vice versa. The scientist, on the other hand, would have to look at a lot more data before pronouncing anything.

This is why it is dangerous to allow the media to drive scientific debates. Most of the people in the media do not have scientific backgrounds. Apart from the fact that the media does have its own agenda to consolidate power, it is also not equipped for these debates. Unfortunately, when the media becomes too powerful, and all experts bow to it, it will be difficult to keep these critical debates within the scientific community away from the influence of the media

Current models of climate change show the Earth warming with humans being responsible for it. We should trust science for it represents our best knowledge on any subject. However, as Matthew Yglesias pointed out during the coronavirus debates, "While expertise is important, turning 'the experts' and 'the science' into false gods could create a backlash cycle of unrealistic expectations and dashed hopes."[68]

Climate predictions are very tricky, and it is very important to remain humble. Consider the following predictions made in the past.

A British newspaper, the *Independent*, carried a headline in 2000 that said, "Snow falls are now just a thing of the past."[69] The article was written by Charles Onians. It is not known if Onians is a scientist, but he quoted Dr. David Viner, a scientist of the Climate Research Unit of the University of East Anglia. Dr. Viner said, "Within a few years winter snowfall will become a rare and exciting event. Children just aren't going to know what snow is." Of course, at the time of the prediction in 2000, there was very little snowfall in the UK. Those "children" in 2000 are now well in their thirties and still seeing snow!

The *Salon* newspaper of October 23, 2001, quotes author and journalist Bob Reiss, who claimed that Dr. James E. Hansen told him in 1988 that part of New York would be under water by 2018.[70] Dr. Hansen was a NASA scientist and a leading expert on climate change. He was the scientist who predicted the greenhouse effect before the US Congress.[71] Clearly that prediction too did not pan out. The important climate debate is best served when it is left in the hands of scientists, not the media.

Another instance that shows how a powerful media can negatively affect society is the Mueller investigation. After two years of investigation, special counsel Robert Mueller's investigation into the allegations of Russian meddling in the 2016 US presidential elections found no proof that Donald Trump's campaign colluded with Russia.[72]

The media had pushed a story that Donald Trump won the 2016 election because Russia had helped him. The allegations were so widely reported and believed in the media that a special counsel was appointed to investigate the allegations. Throughout the two years that the investigation went on, the media consistently brought on "experts" who claimed that evidence for the Russia-Trump collusion was so damning that the president and his former campaign would be found guilty of crimes.

The story should not even have been taken seriously. The material for the basis of the allegation was found to have originated from somebody working for candidate Hillary Clinton. Allegations in the material could not be proved. Yet because the media wanted this investigation, with the hope that perhaps the president could have been removed from office, two years and a lot of resources were spent concentrating on a bogus story.

Of all the negative consequences of the rising media power, there is none more troubling that when the media enables governments to start unnecessary wars that eventually devastate lives of ordinary citizens. Wars traumatize nations.

Joseph O'Donnell, a US Marines photographer, was sent to document the immediate aftermath of the air raids of firebombs and atomic bombs in Japan in 1945. One of his iconic photographs is that of a Japanese boy standing at attention after having brought his dead younger brother to a cremation pyre.[73] Taken in 1945, the picture came to be known as *The Boy Standing by the Crematory*.

Speaking in an interview about this picture, O'Donnell said:

I saw a boy about ten years old walking by. He was carrying a baby on his back. In those days in Japan, we often saw children playing with their little brothers or sisters on their backs, but this boy was clearly different. I could see that he had come to this place for a serious reason. He was wearing no shoes. His face was hard. The little head was tipped back as if the baby were fast asleep. The boy stood there for five or ten minutes.

The men in white masks walked over to him and quietly began to take off the rope that was holding the baby. That is when I saw that the baby was already dead. The men held the body by the hands and feet and placed it on the fire. The boy stood there straight without moving, watching the flames. He was biting his lower lip so hard that it shone with blood. The flame burned low like the sun going down. The boy turned around and walked silently away.[74]

The consequences of war can devastate nations for many generations. In the 1980s, during the civil war in Mozambique, the rebels brutally fought government forces in a guerrilla war. The guerrilla rebels, known as RENAMO, used gruesome tactics in the battle. Thousands of refugees crossed the Malawi/

Mozambique border into Malawi, bringing with them many horrible stories of atrocities committed by RENAMO on civilians.

In one such horrible atrocity, refugees recounted a story of a woman whose husband was a government supporter. Brutal RENAMO guerrilla soldiers came to their house at night, killed the husband, cut him up, and gave his liver to the wife to cook and eat at gunpoint. This was one of many gruesome accounts by refugees. There was no way to verify it. But given RENAMO's brutal war tactics, there was little doubt in its veracity.

Wars are never sexy. They are terrible, traumatic, and devastating, except of course when you watch the American media. The media has a history of romanticizing, enabling, and encouraging successful administrations to start wars.

Starting in 2010, a series of protests and rebellions spread across the Arab world deposing well-known dictators, one by one. By 2011, the protests and rebellions had reached Libya and its leader Muammar Gaddafi. Gaddafi always had a somewhat controversial relationship with the United States, in particular, and the West in general. Gaddafi had been implicated in many terrorist incidents in the West, including the 1988 bombing of Pan Am Flight 103 over Lockerby, Scotland.

As the rebels fought against Gaddafi's forces, the North Atlantic Treaty Organization (NATO) started discussing the possibility of sending soldiers to Libya to help the rebels depose Gaddafi. While the UK and France were ready to provide the air power needed to depose Gaddafi, US president Barack Obama appeared reluctant to join the war, perhaps because of his African roots. African nations, led by South Africa and supported by other world figures, were strongly opposed to the external involvement in Libya.

CNN's Anderson Cooper dedicated his program to providing a very grim picture of atrocities allegedly being committed in Libya. Sometimes Cooper would bring on his program voices of anonymous people claiming to have been eyewitness to the atrocities. The general narrative by the media was that Gaddafi was bombing his own people and that NATO must go into Libya very quickly to depose him and liberate innocent civilians before things got worse.

On March 4, 2011, Cooper started his program by saying:

Moammar Gadhafi is cracking down, cracking down and killing his own people again, using deadly force on the streets of Tripoli and the city of Zawiyah and cracking down on reporters who aren't cooperating, taking away their cameras, trying to blind the world to what is happening.

But the videos keep coming. This newly uploaded cell phone video is report-edly from Zawiyah. On YouTube, it says it's from today. We cannot independently verify that, however. We do know from numerous reports today that government forces, which had surrounded the city, moved in hard on protesters who were armed with sticks and rocks and in some cases guns.

Gadhafi forces were said to use mortar and machine gun fire. Watch. Again, we cannot independently verify exactly when this video was taken. One witness we spoke with said what happened was indescribable, a local doctor reporting 15 dead and upwards of 200 wounded.

There's a river of blood, he says, running through his hospital. The regime, meantime, saying they have recaptured the city. The exact word they used was liberated, which, again, we cannot confirm. Remember, according to the Gadhafi regime, the Libyan people are all behind him, but are being held hostage by a small number of al Qaeda terrorists. That's his viewpoint.[75]

This reporting was meant to convince the American people of the advantages of war against Libya and force the reluctant American administration to move forward. On the same program, CNN analyst Fareed Zakaria wanted the CIA to "start looking into covert actions that can fund the rebels, that can provide food, logistics, weaponry. And if Gadhafi realizes this—and believe me, we don't need to advertise it—he would realize, he will see, the people around him will see he can't win.[76] The key here is to make him understand that he is not going to be able to survive and that therefore, what he needs to do now is negotiate the terms of his departure," Zakaria said.

France and Britain eventually provided the air power that led to the defeat of Gaddafi. The rebels captured Gaddafi and killed him. Pictures of his gruesome death were shown all over the world.[77] To this date, no evidence has been found that at the time Gaddafi was using military planes to bomb his own people. Anderson Cooper and his colleagues in the media have not even bothered to explain where they got that information and why it appears to have been wrong.

Because Gaddafi had good relations with sub-Saharan countries and had invited many black Africans to work in Libya, his death was followed by the targeting of black Africans in Libya. Black Africans were hunted and killed, with some of them being accused of being mercenaries. The American television networks that were so eager to have NATO intervene in Libya to depose Gaddafi for the sake of the people, were now silent.[78]

As Al Jazeera reported, dozens of workers from sub-Saharan Africa were killed, and hundreds were in hiding, as angry mobs of antigovernment protesters hunted them down.[79] Reuters reported that "dead men of African origin have been a common sight since the uprising, as has been the sight of ill treatment of Africans by Libyan anti-Gaddafi fighters."[80] Hein de Haas, a senior fellow with the International Migration Institute, wondered why nobody seemed "concerned about the plight of sub-Saharan African migrants in Libya? As victims of racism and ruthless exploitation, they are Libya's most vulnerable immigrant population."[81]

Another war the media was obsessed about was the Iraq War. In the run-up to the second Iraq War in 2013, the George W. Bush administration claimed that Iraq had weapons of mass destruction, and that it was, therefore, important to disarm Iraq. The evidence given was at best suspect, but the media failed to ask tough questions of the administration, and instead supported the war. One memorable interaction[82] between journalists and the then secretary of defense Donald Rumsfeld shows how little resistance the administration met as it pushed through its war agenda:

> Reporter 1: "There are reports that there is no evidence of direct report between Bagdad and some of these terrorist organizations."
> Rumsfeld: "There are known knowns; there are things we know we know. We also know there are known unknowns, that is to say we know there are things we do not know. But there are also unknown unknowns, the ones we don't know we don't know."
> Reporter 2: "Excuse me, but is this an unknown unknown?"
> Rumsfeld: "I am not gonna say which it is."

News networks spent more time endearing themselves to the administration than scrutinizing it. Eason Jordan, CNN chief news executive, boasted that he had visited the Pentagon with a list of possible military commentators, asked officials there if that was a good list to have, and got a thumbs up on all of them.[83]

When then Secretary of State Colin Powell went before the UN Security Council to present evidence of weapons of mass destruction, the media cheered the evidence as very strong. Everything was taken at face value.

Colin Powell's evidence was full of holes. He started his testimony by claiming that due to the sensitive and technical nature of the evidence, he could not tell everything he knew. "I cannot tell you everything that we know. But what I can share with you, when combined with what all of us have learned over the years, is deeply troubling,"[84] he said. Powell went ahead and played audios that he claimed were by Iraqi soldiers. He also showed aerial photos and some models of what he said were Iraqi vehicles for moving weapons of mass destruction around.

Nothing Powell presented the Security Council directly tied to Saddam Hussein or Iraq on its own. There was no evidence to show that the audios were real and not just enactments. There was no evidence to prove that the vehicles shown in the testimony were indeed Iraqi vehicles. Unfortunately, journalists instead praised Powell's evidence and described it as very powerful.

After many years of fighting in Iraq, the United States finally admitted that there were no weapons of mass destruction in Iraq. This was a war that would almost not have happened if the media had not either supported or enabled it. Yet it killed and wounded thousands of Iraqis and Americans, not to mention it took billions of dollars that could have been used back in America to solve growing societal problems.

Democracies require a free and independent media to inform the public and shed light on activities of government. In America's case, a previously unknown phenomenon appears to have developed. The media, which was intended to check the powerful, has itself become the most powerful institution. Whenever an entity becomes too powerful to check, democracy is threatened.

Never before was it more necessary for citizens to speak out about their views without intimidation. Schools have a very big role in this by developing curricula that teach and encourage students to be independent thinkers and custodians of democracy. School campuses should also be places where freedom of thought and expression is encouraged without bounds.

NOTES

1. Wulfsohn, Joseph A. "Joe Rogan forces Dr. Sanjay Gupta to admit CNN shouldn't have called his COVID treatment 'horse dewormer,'" Fox News, October 13, 2021. https://www.foxnews.com/media/joe-rogan-dr-sanjay-gupta-cnn-ivermectin; "The Joe Rogan Experience," Podcast, October 13, 2021.

2. Rogers, K. "Sanjay Gupta," *Encyclopedia Britannica*, October 19, 2021. https://www.britannica.com/biography/Sanjay-Gupta.

3. Susan Jaffe. "Legal challenges threaten Biden's COVID-19 vaccine rule," *The Lancet* 398, no. 10314 (2021): 1863–64, ISSN 0140–6736, https://doi.org/10.1016/S0140-6736(21)02537-X. https://www.sciencedirect.com/science/article/pii/S014067362102537X

4. Hoffman, Jason. "Trump on America surpassing 200,000 coronavirus deaths: "Well, I think it's a shame,'" CNN, September 22, 2020. https://www.cnn.com/world/live-news/coronavirus-pandemic-09-22-20-intl/h_1048708bd08c30a0a82156f2f166b094

5. O'Donnell, Jayne. "Top disease official: Risk of coronavirus in USA is 'minuscule'; skip mask and wash hands," *USA Today*, February 17, 2020. https://www.usatoday.com/story/news/health/2020/02/17/nih-disease-official-anthony-fauci-risk-of-coronavirus-in-u-s-is-minuscule-skip-mask-and-wash-hands/4787209002/

6. Reuters Staff. "Fact check: Outdated video of Fauci saying "there's no reason to be walking around with a mask,'" Reuters, October 8, 2020, 8:31 AM EST. https://www.reuters.com/article/uk-factcheck-fauci-outdated-video-masks/fact-checkoutdated-video-of-fauci-saying-theres-no-reason-to-be-walking-around-with-a

-mask-idUSKBN26T2TR; *60 Minutes.* "March 2020: Dr. Anthony Fauci talks with Dr. Jon LaPook about Covid-19," CBS, March 8, 2020. https://www.youtube.com/watch?v=PRa6t_e7dgI

7. Weiter, Taylor. "'Here we go with theater': Rand Paul, Dr. Fauci share heated exchange over vaccine, double masks," ABC WHAS11, April 19, 2021. https://www.whas11.com/article/news/politics/rand-paul-fauci-double-masks-covid-reinfection/417-469a2339-f843-412f-b940-4d407d9a21bc

8. Farmer, Brit McCandless. "March 2020: Dr. Anthony Fauci talks with Dr. Jon LaPook about COVID-19," CBS News *60 Minutes Overtime*, March 8, 2020. https://www.cbsnews.com/news/preventing-coronavirus-facemask-60-minutes-2020-03-08/

9. Kelley, Alexandra. "Fauci: Why the public wasn't told to wear masks when the coronavirus pandemic began," *The Hill*, June 16, 2020. https://thehill.com/changing-america/well-being/prevention-cures/502890-fauci-why-the-public-wasnt-told-to-wear-masks

10. Ruiz, Michelle. "For Dr. Anthony Fauci and Dr. Christine Grady, love conquers all," *Vogue*, February 1, 2021. https://www.vogue.com/article/dr-anthony-fauci-and-dr-christine-grady-love-story

11. Adams, Becket. "Frank Luntz is right: Get Fauci off TV," *Washington Examiner*, July 28, 2021, 4:07 PM EST. https://www.washingtonexaminer.com/opinion/frank-luntz-is-right-get-fauci-off-tv

12. Porterfield, Carlie. "Dr. Fauci on GOP criticism: 'Attacks on me, quite frankly, are attacks on science,'" *Forbes*, June 10, 2021. https://www.forbes.com/sites/carlieporterfield/2021/06/09/fauci-on-gop-criticism-attacks-on-me-quite-frankly-are-attacks-on-science/?sh=1fe5812f4542

13. Calisher, Charles, et al. "Statement in support of the scientists, public health professionals, and medical professionals of China combatting COVID-19," *The Lancet* 395, no. 10226 (February 19, 2020): e42–e43, ISSN: 0140–6736. https://doi.org/10.1016/S0140-6736(20)30418-9

14. Calisher, Charles, et al. "Science, not speculation, is essential to determine how SARS-CoV-2 reached humans." *The Lancet* 398, no. 10296 (July 5, 2021): 209–11, ISSN: 0140–6736. https://doi.org/10.1016/S0140-6736(21)01419-7

15. Van Helden, Jacques, et al. "An appeal for an objective, open, and transparent scientific debate about the origin of SARS-CoV-2," *The Lancet* 398, no. 10309 (September 17, 2021): 1402–04, ISSN: 0140–6736. https://doi.org/10.1016/S0140-6736(21)02019-5

16. Viglione, Giuliana. "Four ways Trump has meddled in pandemic science—and why it matters," *Nature*, November 3, 2020. https://www.nature.com/articles/d41586-020-03035-4

17. O'Kane, Caitlin. "Trump listens 'even if we disagree on some things,' Dr. Fauci says in interview about coronavirus task force," CBS News, March 22, 2020. https://www.cbsnews.com/news/coronavirus-trump-fauci-interview-meme-listens-disagree-contradiction-white-house-task-force-press-briefings/; Luscombe, Richard. "Fauci: No evidence anti-malaria drug pushed by Trump works against virus," *The Guardian*, April 6, 2020. https://www.theguardian.com/world/2020/apr/05/coronavirus-fauci-trump-anti-malaria-drug

18. Mehra, M. R., Desai, S. S., Ruschitzka, F., and Patel, A. N. "RETRACTED: Hydroxychloroquine or chloroquine with or without a macrolide for treatment of COVID-19: a multinational registry analysis," *The Lancet*, May 22, 2020. https://doi.org/10.1016/S0140-6736(20)31180-6

19. Adams, Becket. "Frank Luntz is right: Get Fauci off TV," *Washington Examiner*, July 28, 2021, 4:07 PM EST. https://www.washingtonexaminer.com/opinion/frank-luntz-is-right-get-fauci-off-tv

20. Piper, Kelsey. "This coronavirus model keeps being wrong. Why are we still listening to it?," Vox, May 2, 2020. https://www.vox.com/future-perfect/2020/5/2/21241261/coronavirus-modeling-us-deaths-ihme-pandemic

21. Holmdahl, Inga, and Buckee, Caroline. "Wrong but useful—what Covid-19 epidemiologic models can and cannot tell us," *New England Journal of Medicine* 383, no. 4 (2020). https://doi.org/10.1056/NEJMp2016822

22. Biggs A. T., Littlejohn, L. F. "Revisiting the initial COVID-19 pandemic projections," *Lancet Microbe* 2, no. 3 (March 2021): e91–e92. https://doi.org/10.1016/S2666-5247(21)00029-X. Epub 2021 Mar 2. PMID: 33942033; PMCID: PMC8081652

23. World Health Organization (WHO). Twitter post, January 14, 2020, 6:18 AM EST. https://twitter.com/WHO/status/1217043229427761152?s=20

24. World Health Organization (WHO), Twitter post, April 9, 2020, 3:52 PM EST. https://twitter.com/WHO/status/1248353020888440832?s=20

25. Zizo, Christie, and Small, Taurean. "Disease expert: Flu a bigger risk in the US than coronavirus," *Spectrum News* 13 (February 15, 2020), 11:12 AM EST. https://www.mynews13.com/fl/orlando/news/2020/02/15/disease-expert--flu-a-bigger-risk-in-the-us-than-coronavirus

26. Margolin, Josh, and Meek, James Gordon. "Intelligence report warned of coronavirus crisis as early as November," ABC News, April 8, 2020. https://abcnews.go.com/Politics/intelligence-report-warned-coronavirus-crisis-early-november-sources/story?id=70031273

27. Ibid.

28. Casiano, Louis, and Griffin, Jennifer. "Defense official says media reports about November coronavirus intel assessment are false," Fox News, April 8, 2020. https://www.foxnews.com/politics/defense-november-coronavirus-intelligence-assessment-reports-false

29. Cohen, Zachary, Sciutto, Jim, Marquardt, Alex, and Perez, Evan. "US intelligence agencies started tracking coronavirus outbreak in China as early as November," CNN, April 9, 2020. https://www.cnn.com/2020/04/08/politics/intel-agencies-covid-november/index.html

30. Carlson, Tucker. "Tucker Carlson: Coronavirus was largely ignored by impeachment-obsessed media as epidemic began," Fox News, March 14, 2020. https://www.foxnews.com/opinion/tucker-carlson-coronavirus-story-was-ignored-by-media-obsessed-with-impeachment

31. Siegel, Marc. "Op-Ed: The new coronavirus isn't a threat to people in the United States—but flu is," *Los Angeles Times*, January 29, 2020. https://www.latimes.com/opinion/story/2020-01-29/coronavirus-no-threat-to-americans-but-flu-is

32. Dingwall, Robert. "We should deescalate the war on the coronavirus," Wired, January 29, 2020. https://www.wired.com/story/opinion-we-should-deescalate-the -war-on-the-coronavirus/

33. McClurg, Lesley. "The flu is still a bigger health threat in the U.S. than novel coronavirus," KQED, January 29, 2020. https://www.kqed.org/science/1956289/the -flu-is-a-bigger-health-threat-in-the-u-s-than-novel-coronavirus

34. Yeung, Jessie. "As the coronavirus spreads, fear is fueling racism and xeno- phobia," CNN, January 31, 2020. https://www.cnn.com/2020/01/31/asia/wuhan -coronavirus-racism-fear-intl-hnk/index.html

35. Ducharme, Jamie. "Want to protect yourself from coronavirus? Do the same things you do every winter." *Time*, January 31, 2020. https://time.com/5775359/ coronavirus-prevention-tips/

36. Bernstein, Lenny. "Get a grippe, America. The flu is a much bigger threat than coronavirus, for now," *Washington Post*, February 1, 2020. https://www .washingtonpost.com/health/time-for-a-reality-check-america-the-flu-is-a-much -bigger-threat-than-coronavirus-for-now/2020/01/31/46a15166-4444-11ea-b5fc -eefa848cde99_story.html

37. Henry, Megan, and Hauck, Grace. "Coronavirus is scary, but the flu is deadlier, more widespread," *USA Today*, February 1, 2020. https://www.usatoday.com/story /news/health/2020/02/01/coronavirus-flu-deadlier-more-widespread-than-wuhan -china-virus/4632508002/

38. DiFlorio, Anthony. "Why are we panicked about coronavirus—and calm about the flu?" *The Hill*, February 4, 2020. https://thehill.com/changing-america/well-being /prevention-cures/481257-why-are-we-panicked-about-coronavirus-and-calm

39. Daly, Michael. "The virus killing U.S. kids isn't the one dominating the headlines," Daily Beast, February 6, 2020. https://www.thedailybeast.com/flu-not -coronavirus-is-the-virus-killing-us-kids-like-luca-calanni

40. WICS/WRSP Staff. "Experts warn flu is greater risk than coronavirus," WICS/WRSP, February 13, 2020. https://newschannel20.com/news/local/experts -warn-flu-greater-risk-than-coronavirus

41. Associated Press Staff. "Is the new virus more 'deadly' than flu? Not exactly," Associated Press, February 18, 2020. https://apnews.com/article/ap-top-news-health -china-virus-outbreak-death-rates-6f7d691099b499bbf38fdfe7875126e0

42. England, Bob, and Humble, Will. "New coronavirus is likely to go pandemic, but that's no reason to panic or overreact," AZ Central, February 25, 2020. https:// www.azcentral.com/story/opinion/op-ed/2020/02/25/coronavirus-may-seem-scarier -than-flu-but-lets-not-overreact/4860362002/

43. "Jeff Zucker named new president of CNN Worldwide," CNN, November 29, 2012. https://www.cnn.com/2012/11/29/us/jeff-zucker-cnn-president/index.html

44. Byers, Dylan. "CNN to produce Hillary Clinton film," Politico, July 29, 2013. https://www.politico.com/blogs/media/2013/07/cnn-to-produce-hillary-clinton-film -169427

45. Levin, Gary. "NBC to air Hillary Clinton miniseries," *USA Today*, July 27, 2013. https://www.usatoday.com/story/life/tv/2013/07/27/hillary-clinton-miniseries -nbc/2592431/

46. Camia, Catalina, and Levin, Gary. "CNN, NBC cancel Hillary Clinton film projects," *USA Today*, September 30, 2013. https://www.usatoday.com/story/onpolitics/2013/09/30/hillary-clinton-cnn-documentary/2895209/

47. Memmott, Mark. "Republicans to CNN and NBC: No debates for you," NPR, August 13, 2013. https://www.npr.org/sections/thetwo-way/2013/08/16/212643382/republicans-to-cnn-and-nbc-no-debates-for-you

48. Zito, Salena. "Stumped by Trump's success? Take a drive outside US cities," *New York Post*, August 22, 2016. https://nypost.com/2016/08/22/stumped-by-trumps-success-take-a-drive-outside-us-cities/

49. Bump, Philip. "Your critique that FiveThirtyEight misfired on the 2016 race is wrong," *Washington Post*, September 27, 2017. https://www.washingtonpost.com/news/politics/wp/2017/09/27/your-critique-that-fivethirtyeight-misfired-on-the-2016-race-is-wrong/

50. MSNBC. "Joe: 2016 election results a 'complete earthquake,'" MSNBC *Morning Joe*, November 9, 2016. https://www.youtube.com/watch?v=VgYphOJ7qiw

51. Ibid.

52. "Polling expert, who promised to 'eat a bug' if Trump won, gulps cricket on CNN," CBS San Francisco Bay Area Channel, November 12, 2016. https://sanfrancisco.cbslocal.com/2016/11/12/princeton-polling-expert-promised-to-eat-a-bug-if-trump-won-eats-cricket-cnn/

53. Silver, Nate. "The media has a probability problem," FiveThirtyEight, September 21, 2017. https://fivethirtyeight.com/features/the-media-has-a-probability-problem/?ex_cid=2016-forecast

54. Ibid

55. Silver, Nate. "There really was a liberal media bubble," FiveThirtyEight, March 10, 2017. https://fivethirtyeight.com/features/there-really-was-a-liberal-media-bubble/

56. Vogel, Kenneth P., and Isenstadt, Alex. "How did everyone get it so wrong?" Politico, November 9, 2016. https://www.politico.com/story/2016/11/how-did-everyone-get-2016-wrong-presidential-election-231036

57. "Roy Spencer—U.S. AMSR-E Science Team Leader," NASA Aqua Project Science. https://aqua.nasa.gov/content/roy-spencer-us-amsr-e-science-team-leader

58. "Mark Hertsgaard," Wikipedia. https://en.wikipedia.org/wiki/Mark_Hertsgaard

59. "Piers Morgan—What is man's role in climate change?" November 11, 2011. https://www.youtube.com/watch?v=kt9AKQduIoU

60. Ibid.

61. Wolpert, Lewis, The Unnatural Nature of Science (Cambridge: Harvard University Press, 1992).

62. Ibid.

63. Ibid.

64. "StarChild Question of the Month for February 2003," NASA Goddard Space Flight Center, 2003. https://starchild.gsfc.nasa.gov/docs/StarChild/questions/question54.html

65. Ibid.

66. Ibid.

67. Ibid.

68. Yglesias, Matthew. "The 'experts' don't know everything. They can't," Vox, April 18, 2020. https://www.vox.com/2020/4/18/21221202/listen-to-experts-science

69. Onians, Charles. "Snowfalls are now just a thing of the past," *Independent*, March 20, 2000. https://web.archive.org/web/20150912124604/http:/www.independent.co.uk/environment/snowfalls-are-now-just-a-thing-of-the-past-724017.html

70. Hansen, Suzy. "Stormy weather," Salon, October 23, 2001. https://web.archive.org/web/20110202162233/https:/www.salon.com/books/int/2001/10/23/weather/

71. Shabecoff, Philip. "Global warming has begun, expert tells Senate," Salon, June 24, 1988. https://www.nytimes.com/1988/06/24/us/global-warming-has-begun-expert-tells-senate.html/

72. Johnston, Abby, and Miller, Leila. "The Mueller investigation, explained," PBS *Frontline*, March 25, 2019. https://www.pbs.org/wgbh/frontline/article/the-mueller-investigation-explained-2/

73. "A Japanese boy standing at attention after having brought his dead younger brother to a cremation pyre, 1945," Rare Historical Photos, November 23, 2021. https://rarehistoricalphotos.com/japanese-boy-standing-attention-brought-dead-younger-brother-cremation-pyre-1945/

74. Ibid.

75. *Anderson Cooper 360*, CNN Transcripts, March 4, 2011, 10:00 PM EST. https://transcripts.cnn.com/show/acd/date/2011-03-04/segment/01

76. Ibid.

77. Gaynor, Tim, and Zargoun, Taha. "Gaddafi caught like 'rat' in a drain, humiliated and shot," Reuters, October 21, 2011. https://www.reuters.com/article/us-libya-gaddafi-finalhours/gaddafi-caught-like-rat-in-a-drain-humiliated-and-shot-idUS-TRE79K43S20111021; Williams, David. "Who shot Gaddafi? New video shows blood pouring from dictator immediately before death but mystery surrounds coup de grace," *Daily Mail*, October 21, 2011. https://www.dailymail.co.uk/news/article-2051361/GADDAFI-DEAD-VIDEO-Dictator-begs-life-summary-execution.html

78. "African migrants targeted in Libya," Al Jazeera, February 28, 2011. https://www.aljazeera.com/news/2011/2/28/african-migrants-targeted-in-libya

79. Ibid.

80. Abbas, Mohammed. "African workers live in fear after Gaddafi overthrow," Reuters, August 31, 2011. https://www.reuters.com/article/us-libya-africans/african-workers-live-in-fear-after-gaddafi-overthrow-idUSTRE77U6O520110831

81. "African migrants targeted in Libya," Al Jazeera.

82. "War Made Easy," YouTube, September 11, 2014. https://www.youtube.com/watch?v=jPJs8x-BKYA

83. Ibid.

84. "Full text of Colin Powell's speech," *The Guardian*, February 5, 2003. https://www.theguardian.com/world/2003/feb/05/iraq.usa

Chapter 4

How the Media
Influences Religion

The Christian world celebrates December 25 every year as the day of the birth of Jesus Christ, who is considered by Christians to be the Son of God. However, according to history, the day has nothing to do with the actual birth of Jesus. One legend says that it was Pope Julius I of the Roman Catholic Church who instituted December 25 as Christmas Day. He wanted to convert and absorb pagans who, at the time, celebrated the winter solstice as a symbol of the resurgence of the sun—the casting away of winter and the heralding of the rebirth of spring and summer.[1]

Some early Christians opposed Christmas. They did not believe that it was biblical to celebrate the birth of Christ on a pagan holiday. Over the years, that opposition has melted away, and today, almost the whole of Christendom celebrates Christmas with festivals, special church programs, and of course, commercial gifts.

The manner in which Christians first opposed Christmas but then later embraced it is a metaphor for the evolution of Christianity. Oftentimes in history, Christians have rejected certain practices, only to embrace them later under the influence of the secular world. It is, therefore, not surprising that such an influenceable religion has fallen victim to the powerful influence of the secular media. Positions Christians have taken over the years, on abortion, same-sex marriage, and ordination of women appear to have been influenced more by the media than the Holy Spirit as claimed by the church.

The idea that the changing positions in the Christian world are influenced by the changing perceptions in the general public is not largely disputed in Christendom. Church leaders often talk about it. In April 2005, a day before his election as Pope Benedict XVI, Cardinal Joseph Ratzinger warned against what he called relativism, "the tendency to allow oneself to be led here and there by any wind of doctrine," a practice he said was seen by the world as "the only behavior abreast of the times."[2]

In a free society, there should be nothing wrong with same-sex marriage or abortion. The point of discussing these hot-button issues is not to show that churches are wrong, or vice versa, when they change their initial positions under the influence of the media. Rather, the point is to show that the media in America is so powerful that it influences every aspect of life, including religion.

Churches are so afraid of the media that, these days, it is difficult to get a straight answer from church leaders on any of these hot-button issues. Ask them what their church's position is on same-sex marriage, abortion, or ordination of women, and you will get a long nonanswer. There are at least three verses in the Bible that make Christians very uncomfortable. Christians used to trumpet these verses in public, but with changing public perceptions and political correctness, the church does not know how to deal with these passages anymore.

The first passage is found in Genesis 2:18–22 with emphasis on verse 22. The passage says:[3]

> The Lord God said, "It is not good for the man to be alone. I will make a helper suitable for him."
> Now the Lord God had formed out of the ground all the wild animals and all the birds in the sky. He brought them to the man to see what he would name them; and whatever the man called each living creature, that was its name. So, the man gave names to all the livestock, the birds in the sky and all the wild animals.
> But for Adam no suitable helper was found. So, the Lord God caused the man to fall into a deep sleep; and while he was sleeping, he took one of the man's ribs and then closed up the place with flesh. Then the Lord God made a woman from the rib he had taken out of the man, and he brought her to the man.

The passage seems to suggest that God created man—Adam—first. And when God saw that Adam was lonely or had no helper, he decided to create the woman for him. Christians used to have to no problems with that logic. However, these days Christians struggle, especially under the gaze of the media, to interpret or defend the passage.

Another controversial passage is Leviticus 20:13. The passage states:[4]

> If a man has sexual relations with a man as one does with a woman, both of them have done what is detestable. They are to be put to death; their blood will be on their own heads.

It is quite a gruesome verse. Yet Christians used to have no problems with that passage. In some parts of the world, they still do not. In America, however, Bible-believing Christians have a difficult time explaining this verse. Ask any

Christian leader to explain the verse on national television; you are likely to get a nonanswer.

The other passage is found in the New Testament in 1 Timothy 2:12. The Apostle Paul, writing to Timothy, said:[5] "I do not permit a woman to teach or to assume authority over a man; she must be quiet."

This is another controversial verse that seems to suggest that women should not be leaders or teachers in churches.

Whatever these passages mean, modern Christians appear not to have yet figured out how to deal with them. Sometimes, Christians interpret these passages one way within their local church walls when the media is not watching, but then interpret them the other way in public when the media is watching. The bottom line is that the church is very afraid of the media. The media has noticed this vulnerability and tends to exploit it as much as possible.

The media, not least the movie industry, has figured out that the best way to influence the Christian church is to change public perceptions on hot-button issues. Once society is influenced on these issues, the church changes its positions to suit societal thinking. The church does not want to be perceived as discriminatory or political, and risk either losing members or tax-exempt status. So, the church finds ways of justifying its changing positions.

Public perceptions can be changed effectively though movies and the television. One of the things new immigrants to America notice immediately, upon arrival in the country, is the manner in which Americans are very obsessed with movies, and the way movies affect American people's thinking. Only in America can an argument be settled by saying, "This point is true . . . have you seen this movie? That's what happened in that movie," as if the movie was not fiction.

Of course, those who point out the power of the media, especially the movie industry, in influencing attitudes in the general public are often met with sarcasm and mockery that they are being conspiracy theorists. In reality, the idea that the media influences the general public is a well-documented science.

The Norman Lear Center of the Annenberg Center of the University of Southern California (USC) seeks to influence the entertainment industry on a number of important issues affecting the society. The center has also developed techniques to quantifiably show the impact of certain information in movies and television shows on the audience.[6] According to the USC Annenberg Center, "the Norman Lear Center is a multidisciplinary research and public policy center studying and shaping the impact of entertainment and media on society."[7]

Under their Hollywood, Health and Society initiative, the Norman Lear Center was able to show how the documentary *Food Inc.* impacted the people who watched it.[8] Quantifiably, the center was able to show that viewers of *Food Inc.* were more likely to encourage their friends and colleagues to learn more about food safety. They were also more likely to shop at their local farmers market and eat healthy.[9]

Perhaps the most interesting initiative of the Norman Lear Center is the Media Impact Project sponsored by the Gates and Knight Foundations. The objective of the Media Impact Project is to act as a global hub "for collecting, developing, and sharing approaches for measuring the impact of media in order to better understand the role that media plays in changing knowledge, attitudes and behavior among individuals and communities."[10] The data is, among others, used to help the Knight and Gates Foundations make data-driven decisions as they seek to impact the world on a dozen important public issues.[11]

The director of the Norman Lear Center, Martin Kaplan, describes how the center's donor—Norman Lear—kept insisting that as part of their efforts to influence society on climate change, they needed "to have a show that has lots of viewers and has a character who is a total pain in the ass about climate change. And the character he thought would best do that is Manny, the kid, on *Modern Family*."[12] So, it is true that rich and connected people can influence society through the movies and television shows they make.

The Hollywood industry itself is very particular in making sure that it toes a liberal line. While interviewing television executives for his book *Primetime Propaganda*, Ben Shapiro was shocked at how TV executives in Hollywood were prepared to use their clout to advance a liberal political agenda in movies and television shows.[13] In these interviews, television executives openly demonstrated their hatred of conservatives, describing conservatives in very derogatory terms. Most of them agreed that the Hollywood movie industry was left leaning, and that they would love to keep it that way.

The shocking revelations in Shapiro's book prompted the Hollywood Caucus for Producers, Writers & Directors to pass a resolution to amend the organization's charter to stand against discrimination based on political ideology.[14] Mell Flynn, president of the Hollywood Congress of Republicans, agreed that there is a lot of discrimination against Republicans in Hollywood. People get fired from jobs after making their conservative political affiliation known.[15] For example, after posting a tweet to criticize President Barack Obama, conservative actor James Woods said he expected to struggle to find work in the liberal Hollywood industry.[16]

Speaking on *The Faulkner Focus*, Antonio Sabato Jr., alongside actor Kevin Sorbo and country music artist John Rich, said that Hollywood elites want to control the minds of everyone and shut down differing political opinions.[17] Sabato told another publication that his Hollywood career effectively ended after publicly supporting candidate Donald Trump. He said he was blacklisted from Hollywood.[18] Sabato said:

I had to sell everything . . . I had to pay all my debts. I was blacklisted. All my representatives left me, from agents to managers to commercial agents. I literally had to move, find a new job to survive and take care of my kids. It's been terrible. It's mind-blowing. It's a disgrace. It's tough, because if you're in that environment in Hollywood and you have something to say that they don't like, they're going to let you know.[19]

When President Trump scheduled a fundraiser in Beverly Hills, Eric McCormack, a star of *Will & Grace*, tweeted, urging the *Hollywood Reporter* to reveal names of those who would be attending so Hollywood would know not to work with them again.[20]

Many people including some liberals condemned this discriminatory behavior. Whoopi Goldberg compared this behavior to the Hollywood blacklists of the McCarthy era. "This is not a good idea, okay? Your idea of who you don't want to work with is your personal business. Do not encourage people to print out lists because the next list that comes out, your name will be on, and then people will be coming after you!"[21] she said.

A lot of movies have been credited with changing public perceptions on many things. For instance, Marco Morini has shown that the change of public perception on same-sex marriage was largely helped by the entertainment industry's efforts to show gay and lesbian characters as more mainstream in their productions.[22] Inclusive advertisements also helped shape public perception.[23]

The Boys in the Band was arguably the first American movie to focus on gay characters.[24] It was released on March 17, 1970. In its review of the movie, *Time* magazine said, "If the situation of the homosexual is ever to be understood by the public, it will be because of the breakthrough made by this humane, moving picture."[25]

Other notable movies include:

- *Cruising* (1980) is a movie about a police detective who goes undercover in the underground S&M gay subculture of New York City to catch a serial killer preying on gay men.[26]
- *Desert Hearts* (1985) is a movie about a divorcing repressed professor of literature who is unexpectedly seduced by a carefree, spirited young lesbian.[27]
- *The Celluloid Closet* (1995) is a documentary about various Hollywood screen depictions of homosexuals and the attitudes behind them throughout the history of North American film.[28]
- In the 1996 movie, *Bound*, tough ex-con Corky and her lover Violet concoct a scheme to steal millions of stashed mob money and pin the blame on Violet's crooked boyfriend Caesar.[29]

- *Boys Don't Cry* came out in 1999. It is a movie about a young man who navigates love, life, and being transgender in rural Nebraska.[30]
- *Angels in America* is a 2003 movie adapted from playwright Tony Kushner's political epic about the AIDS crisis during the mid-1980s and centers the story around a group of disparate but connected individuals.[31]
- *Brokeback Mountain* (2005) is about two male shepherds who develop a sexual and emotional relationship. Their relationship becomes complicated when both of them get married to their respective girlfriends.[32]
- The 2015 movie *Carol* depicts an aspiring photographer who develops an intimate relationship with an older woman in 1950s New York.[33]
- *BPM (Beats Per Minute)* (2017) is a movie about members of the advocacy group ACT UP Paris who demand action by the government and pharmaceutical companies to combat the AIDS epidemic in the early 1990s.[34]
- *Call Me by Your Name* is a 2017 movie about romance that blossoms between a seventeen-year-old student and the older man hired as his father's research assistant in 1980s Italy.[35]

As the movies became popular, so did the rise in support for same-sex marriage. Over the decade, from 2003 to 2013, the rise in support for same-sex marriages was among the largest changes in opinion on any policy issue over this time period.[36]

Gallup has been monitoring the favorability of same-sex marriages among Americans since 1996, when support for same-sex marriage was only 26 percent. By 2021, support for same-sex marriage had shot up to 70 percent.[37] The PEW Research Center provides the proportions of those who support versus oppose same-sex marriages from 2001 onward. According to the PEW data, support for same-sex marriage had been increasing steadily. In 2001, only 35 percent of Americans supported same-sex marriages. By 2019, nearly 61 percent favored it.

The year 2011 was pivotal in that for the first time ever, more Americans supported the idea of same-sex marriage than opposed it.[38] Before 2011, more Americans had opposed same-sex marriage than supported it. The year 2011 is very important because most major Christian churches that changed their positions on same-sex marriages in recent times changed around that year. The churches had gotten the cue that the public had changed its perception on the subject. The churches thus followed the public. This change in public perception was most likely due to the movie industry impact.

In 2004, the Alliance of Baptists adopted the "Statement on Same Sex Marriage" that affirms their support for the rights of all citizens to full marriage equality.[39] In 2005, the United Church of Christ's General Synod voted to legally recognize and advocate in favor of same-sex marriage. Given the autonomous nature of United Church of Christ churches, each congregation may adopt or reject the recommendations of the General Synod.[40]

In July 2012, the General Convention of the Episcopal Church approved a liturgy for blessing same-sex relationships.[41] After the 2015 US Supreme Court decision recognizing same-sex marriage nationwide, the General Convention of the Episcopal Church approved the trial-use marriage rites for use by all couples. A follow-up measure in 2018 sought to ensure same-sex couples had access to those rites in all of the church's domestic dioceses.[42]

In 2014, the General Assembly of the Presbyterian Church (USA) passed a measure that permits ministers and sessions (local church government), "to use their own discernment to conduct same-sex marriage ceremonies where allowed by law." In addition, the General Assembly recommended an amendment to update the description of marriage in the denomination's *Book of Order* so that it would no longer exclude same-sex couples.

Effective June 2015, the amendment to the *Book of Order* updates the description of marriage as "a unique commitment between two people, traditionally a man and a woman." The latter was added during debate of the amendment on the floor of the General Assembly out of respect to the denomination's more conservative members.[43]

The United Methodist Church has maintained that marriage is between a man and a woman. The clergy of the church are prohibited from performing same-sex marriages.[44] However, the issue is still contentious within the church and is expected to be revisited at the church's next General Conference scheduled for August 9 to September 6, 2022.[45]

Even some non-Christian religious bodies like the conservative Jewish movement made changes along the same line. In June 2012, the movement approved a ceremony to allow same-sex couples to marry.[46]

So it is very clear that the church position on this important issue was affected, not by a new understanding of the scripture, but by the pressure of the media through the public that had already changed its perception. The way to influence church positions is to change public perceptions. As public perceptions change, so does the church. This observation is also reflected in another culture war being fought within Christendom—the ordination of women.

For a long time, the Christian church had claimed that only men could lead the church, and that this was based on instructions from God through His holy word, the Bible. Although modern Christian denominations started ordination of women as early as the mid-nineteenth century, a lot of them held back.[47] A wave of feminism in the1960s and 1970s forced some Christian churches to start ordaining women. These included the American Lutheran Church (ALC) and the Lutheran Church in America (LCA), the Metropolitan Community Church, Reform and Reconstructionist Judaism, and the Episcopal Church.[48]

Still other Christian denominations have resisted this pressure. These include the Roman Catholic Church, the Missouri Synod Lutheran Church, the Latter-day Saints, the Southern Baptist Convention, the Seventh-day Adventists, and most of the Orthodox Jews groupings.[49]

Nevertheless, there is continued pressure within these organizations to start ordaining women. The Roman Catholic Church, for instance, continues to state that "the exclusion of women from the priesthood is in accordance with God's plan for His Church."[50]

Surprisingly, proponents of women's ordination in Christendom, while citing some scripture, give the "changing culture" as the argument for doing it. This appeared to have been the case recently when the Seventh-day Adventist Church (SDA) debated the issue of ordination of women at its 60th General Conference session in San Antonio, Texas, in July 2015.[51]

The Seventh-day Adventist Church was formed under the guidance of Ellen White, after a movement led by Baptist preacher William Miller had been disappointed, on October 22, 1844, when Jesus Christ did not return to Earth as Miller had predicted. Today the Seventh-day Adventist Church is the largest religious movement to emerge from the Americas, with more than twenty million members worldwide.[52] It is growing very fast, with most of its members coming from Africa, Latin America, and Asia. The Seventh-day Adventist Church has the second-largest parochial school system in the world, after Roman Catholicism. It has worldwide healthcare, media, and humanitarian operations.[53] These institutions have helped the church to grow very fast.

Apart from their unique belief that the seventh day of the week—Saturday—is Sabbath, Adventists also believe in the unchanging nature of God and His word, and in the coming of Jesus Christ soon. A recent tweet from the Seventh-day Adventist Church headquarters seems to have summarized the Adventist belief in saying, "We have a commitment to Truth that often clashes with culture. That's when we pray for courage, even as we stare into the precipice of rejection and scorn. #Truth #JesusChrist."[54]

In San Antonio, Adventists gathered to settle by vote the question of women's ordination. Opposition to the ordination question was led by Adventist divisions in Africa and South America while support for women's ordination was led by the North American Division (NAD) of the Seventh-day Adventists. In demonstrating biblical support for a "No" vote, opponents spoke of God as unchanging, and of the lack of evidence that Jesus ordained women or that Ellen White was ordained. Opponents asserted that "God does not change . . . Jesus is the truth," and "Jesus did not ordain any woman." They insisted that "Ellen White . . . never was ordained."[55]

Supporters of ordination of women pointed to biblical passages advocating inclusivity to argue that the "Holy Spirit gives to both men and women without regard to gender." They also employed Ellen White's writings, such as her repeated calls for "both men and women to become pastors to the flock of God."[56]

Laura Vance wrote a detailed account of the debate in her paper titled "Rejecting Women's Ordination: The 60th General Conference Session of the Seventh-Day Adventist World Church." Vance points out that it was interesting to observe that "supporters generally accepted the assertion that to ordain women was consistent with cultural changes, especially in Europe and North America."[57] They seemed to have conceded that the support movement was influenced more by culture than anything else.

One of the most influential supporters of women's ordination present at the conference was Jan Paulsen, the former president of the World Seventh-day Adventist Church. His argument for ordination of women appeared to have confirmed this observation when he said, "We are losing so many of our youth and young professionals. They have problems with the moral integrity of the church, and they say, 'Why is the church having problems with this matter? The public does not. It's not a problem to the public. Why should it be to the church?'"[58]

The voting ended in favor of those who opposed the ordination of women. There is no question that the issue has not been settled and will most certainly be revived after the current leader of the church, Ted Wilson, retires. Pastor Wilson is believed to be strongly against ordination of women.[59] When the Seventh-day Adventist Church finally ordains women, it most likely will have been driven by its powerful and rich North American Division which, itself, tends to be very influenceable by public opinion.

The North American Division of the Seventh-day Adventists, popularly known as NAD, has a history of paying close attention to the media before making important decisions. This was quite evident recently in dealing with one of their own clergy, Dr. Eric Walsh. Dr. Walsh was the public health director for the city of Pasadena, California. He was also the associate pastor for the Altadena Seventh-day Adventist Church within the NAD. In many ways, Dr. Walsh was a highflyer—an up-and-coming young Adventist professional. He was raised in the church and was mostly trained in the church's institutions.

Dr. Walsh got his bachelor's degree from Oakwood University, an African American Adventist college. He then obtained a masters and doctorate in public health from the Loma Linda University, another flagship university of the church. He also obtained a medical doctorate from the University of Miami. Dr. Walsh first worked on the faculty at Loma Linda University. He then became medical director for the Family Health Division of the Orange

County Health Care Agency in California. He also served as the medical director for the five county jails in Orange County. He became the health director of the Pasadena Health Department in 2010.

As director for the city of Pasadena Health Department, Dr. Walsh worked with the city to put in place city ordinances against smoking and unhealthy foods. He set up a dental clinic for people with HIV/AIDS. He received rave reviews for his work in Pasadena. The *Los Angeles Times* acknowledged that Pasadena was of one of the better run cities in southern California.[60]

During this time, he also served as the associate pastor of the Altadena Seventh-day Adventist Church. He loved preaching the Adventist message. After all, he was brought up in the church. In the Adventist Church, an associate pastor generally assists the senior pastor, who is the main pastor of a local church. However, for some six months at the Altadena SDA Church, Dr. Walsh was the only pastor.

His speaking talent was evident. He was invited to speak at many functions—both religious and secular—within the city of Pasadena. In 2012, he was the guest speaker at the Pasadena Mayor's Prayer Breakfast. His speech at the prayer breakfast, still on YouTube, was well received.[61] He spoke about the need to reduce inequality in income and education, offering access to housing and safe environments, and caring for children and the elderly.[62] He got a standing ovation at the end of it. Media reviews were also very positive.[63]

As his name became well known, he was invited to serve in many additional capacities. He became the president of the California Academy of Preventive Medicine. Nationally, he also served two administrations—of George W. Bush and Barack Obama—on the Presidential Advisory Council on HIV/AIDS. Some even speculated that he would he end up as US surgeon general.

On May 9, 2014, Dr. Walsh was invited to be the commencement speaker at Pasadena City College (PCC). He was to be the replacement speaker. Originally, the school had invited Dustin Lance Black to speak. However, the college withdrew that invitation after a video surfaced purporting to show Black having sex with a boyfriend.[64] The PCC administrators were afraid that the sex tape would give their college a bad name, coming immediately after another scandal the previous year, when a PCC professor had invited adult film stars to speak in a class on pornography and admitted to affairs with his students.[65]

Dustin Lance Black was a popular Oscar-winning Hollywood screenwriter. The decision to disinvite him was not very popular with his supporters among the PCC students. The students went online to dig up any trash they could find on Dr. Walsh. If somebody could discredit their favorite speaker just because of something online, they might as well find something on Walsh.

The students probably did not find the kind of dirt they were looking for. But they found something more numbing; they found sermons Dr. Walsh had been delivering in his church on Saturdays every weekend. Seventh-day Adventists worship on Saturdays, the day they call the Sabbath.

According to the *Los Angeles Times*, Dr. Walsh, in his church sermons, preached that he did not believe in evolution, but in creation. He was quoted as saying, "The idea that the Earth evolved over millions of years is a farce. It's not true. It couldn't have happened that way. . . . There is no evidence that we evolved. Where are all the half-things in the world? Where are the animals that are still evolving?"[66]

The *Los Angeles Times* said, among other things, that Dr. Walsh equated the Catholic Church's veneration of Mary, the mother of Jesus, with pagan idolatry. He claimed that the statues of the Virgin of Guadalupe were a lie of Satan. He also described Buddhists who offer food and flowers at altars as engaging in pagan idolatry.[67] The *Pasadena Star News* also alleged that, in those sermons in his church, he had said some incendiary things about other religions, denominations, lifestyles, and the entertainment world.[68]

As soon as the sermons were identified, excerpts of the sermons were published by *Out* magazine, the *Pasadena Star News*, the *Los Angeles Times*, and many other news outlets in southern California. The sermons caused a firestorm and outrage in Southern California.[69] Dr. Walsh withdrew himself as commencement speaker at PCC. And two days later, Pasadena city manager Michael Beck placed Dr. Walsh on a paid administrative leave.[70]

Shortly afterward, Dr. Walsh was forced to resign from his position with the City of Pasadena. He later got a job offer to be the district health officer for Northwest Georgia. That offer was rescinded after the employer heard of the reports in California. In the next couple of years, Dr. Walsh lost his livelihood, his home, and his family. His wife divorced him.

Dr. Walsh was later offered legal representation by the First Liberty Institute of Dallas, Texas. They filed a religious discrimination suit again the state of Georgia. Jeremy Dys of the First Liberty Institute stated: "No one in this country should be fired from their job for something that was said in a church from a pulpit during a sermon. If the government is allowed to fire someone over what he said in his sermons, they can come after any of us for our beliefs on anything. The state has no business snooping around in a pastor's study looking for sermons."[71]

Preachers of some denominations, including the Southern Baptist church and Pentecostals, supported Dr. Walsh's case in Georgia. When the state of Georgia handed him legal papers, requiring him to surrender copies of his sermon notes and transcripts, Dr. Walsh refused. He, standing with the First Liberty attorneys and many preachers on the steps of the Georgia State

Capitol, explained why it was wrong for the government to ask for those sermons.[72]

The state agreed to settle the lawsuit by paying Dr. Walsh $225,000.[73] The surprising part of Dr. Walsh's story is that his own church, the Seventh-day Adventist Church, did not defend him. In fact, they distanced themselves from him as much as possible.

In spite of Dr. Walsh's long service at the Altadena SDA Church, the Southern California Conference of Seventh-day Adventists—a conference within NAD—issued a statement saying that Dr. Walsh "does not hold ministerial credentials from the Adventist Church, does not speak on behalf of the Seventh-day Adventist denomination as far as we know, does not represent his views as anything other than his own." The statement was signed by Betty Cooney.[74]

"The Seventh-day Adventist church has a long history of defending the rights of everyone to believe, practice and express their personal religious convictions. Questions regarding exactly what Dr. Walsh said in previous years, their meaning, intent, and whether or not he has changed his mind, should be addressed to Dr. Walsh," the statement said.

According to Dr Walsh, the decision by the church to abandon him was made high up—not just within the Southern California Conference, perhaps referring to the NAD. When he had tried to contact the Religious Liberty Department at NAD, he was told that, much as that office would have liked to help him, they had been instructed not to be involved in his case.[75] The Adventist Church did not even defend him for believing that the world was created in six days.

Creation, not evolution, is one of the fundamental beliefs of the Seventh-day Adventists. The phrase "seventh day" in the church's name comes from the fact that Seventh-day Adventists believe that God completed his work of creating the world in six literal days, and on the seventh day, he rested. Thus, the seventh day, Saturday, was set apart and blessed as the day of rest—the Sabbath.

The Seventh-day Adventist Church has twenty-eight fundamental beliefs based on the church's "understanding and expression of the teaching of the scripture."[76] The sixth of those fundamental beliefs concerns the creation of the world, and it reads:[77]

> God has revealed in Scripture the authentic and historical account of His creative activity. He created the universe, and in a recent six-day creation the Lord made "the heavens and the earth, the sea, and all that is in them" and rested on the seventh day.

Thus, He established the Sabbath as a perpetual memorial of the work He performed and completed during six literal days that together with the Sabbath constituted the same unit of time that we call a week today.

The first man and woman were made in the image of God as the crowning work of Creation, given dominion over the world, and charged with responsibility to care for it. When the world was finished it was "very good," declaring the glory of God.

As much as Dr. Walsh's sermons appeared controversial and incendiary, they were not different from thousands of sermons delivered every Saturday and Sunday in Christian churches across the United States, including in Seventh-day Adventist churches. They were not so different from the teachings and publications of many Christian denominations in America.

So why did the Adventists distance themselves from Dr. Walsh? Was it because there are no teachings, books, or publications within the Adventist church that mirror some of what Dr. Walsh said?

Whether, as a public official, he should have preached those sermons in his church is a matter that experts on the First Amendment and separation of church and state can argue or disagree. However, what is puzzling is why his own church, the NAD, would not touch him with a ten-foot pole.

The answer here, again, is simple. The church was afraid of what the mighty American press would say. They panicked and decided to distance themselves from a young preacher who had served the church for many years. This, again, is an example of how powerful the press has become in that it not only controls the secular world, but also the religious world.

Most Christian leaders will disagree with this observation. They will argue that the church is always led by the Holy Spirit, and that recent changes in the church are simply a result of a better understanding of the scripture guided by the Holy Spirit. Let us test that line of thought.

According to the Christian church, the Holy Spirit is the third member of the Godhead in the Trinity. As such, the Holy Spirit can be described as a supernatural all-intelligent all-knowing being. If the Christian church is consistently being led by the Holy Spirit, and those outside the Christian church are not, then the church will be ahead of those outside the church in wisdom and knowledge, obviously, because the church would have this all-powerful and all-intelligent being advising it.

The problem with that argument is that almost every change the church has made in recent times, has mirrored changes that had already happened among people outside the church. In other ways, on these hot-button issues, the church appears to always follow in the footsteps of those outside the church. This suggests that, on these hot-button issues, at any point in time, the knowledge and wisdom of those outside the church is more advanced than that of the church. Otherwise, why else would the church always be following in their footsteps?

A church led by the Holy Spirit would exhibit either or both of these two characteristics:

- Characteristic 1: The church would consistently be ahead of those outside the church on these hot-button issues. Because it would have the benefit of being led by the Holy Spirit, the church would know to make the changes before those outside the church do. Thus, issues like same-sex marriages would be adopted by the church before those outside the church adopted them.
- Characteristic 2: The church would behave completely differently from the people outside the church. Thus, on these hot buttons, the church would take positions completely different from positions taken by people outside the church.

The current Christian church cannot be identified with any of these two characteristics. Instead, the pattern is that after arguing for a long time that certain practices are wrong, the church eventually changes its position to be in line with the same people it had been moralizing to all the time.

Thus, it is difficult to argue that the current Christian church is led by the Holy Spirit. Perhaps the church is led more by the "Holy" media than the Holy Spirit.

NOTES

1. Hillerbrand, H. J. "Christmas," *Encyclopedia Britannica*, October 25, 2021. https://www.britannica.com/topic/Christmas; Johnson, David, and Chamberlain, Logan. "Origins of the Christmas holiday," Infoplease, November 15, 2021. https://www.infoplease.com/culture-entertainment/holidays/origins-christmas-holiday

2. Joseph Ratzinger, Cardinal. "Dictatorship of Relativism—Cardinal Ratzinger," Crossroads Initiative, April 18, 2005. https://www.crossroadsinitiative.com/media/articles/dictatorship-of-relativism-cardinal-ratzinger/

3. Gen. 2:18–22 (New International Version).

4. Lev. 20:13 (New International Version).

5. 1 Tim. 2:12 (New International Version).

6. Communication and Marketing Staff. "New program funded to measure media impact and audience engagement," USC Annenberg—School for Communication and Journalism, April 29, 2013. https://annenberg.usc.edu/news/published/new-program-funded-measure-media-impact-and-audience-engagement

7. Ibid.

8. "USC Annenberg Centers: The Norman Lear Center," USC Annenberg Centers—The Norman Lear Center, February 21, 2014. https://www.youtube.com/watch?v=TzzEk-m-6Go

9. Ibid.

10. "Proving that media matters," USC Annenberg—Norman Lear Center. https://www.mediaimpactproject.org/

11. Ibid.

12. Ibid.

13. Bond, Paul. "TV executives admit in taped interviews that Hollywood pushes a liberal agenda (exclusive video)," Hollywood Reporter, June 1, 2011. https://www.hollywoodreporter.com/news/general-news/tv-executives-admit-taped-interviews-193116/

14. Shapiro, Ben. "Hollywood finally admits it discriminates against conservatives—could this be the start of something big?" Fox News, July 13, 2011. https://www.foxnews.com/opinion/hollywood-finally-admits-it-discriminates-against-conservatives-could-this-be-the-start-of-something-big

15. McKay, Hollie. "Criticizing Obama: Does it really get you blacklisted in Hollywood?" Fox News, October 11, 2013. https://www.foxnews.com/entertainment/criticizing-obama-does-it-really-get-you-blacklisted-in-hollywood

16. Ibid.

17. Lanum, Nikolas. "Sabato Jr.: Hollywood elites want to 'control the minds of everyone' and cancel conservatives," Fox News, February 26, 2021. https://www.foxnews.com/media/conservative-actor-sabato-sorbo-rich-hollywood-cancel-culture

18. Toto, Christian. "Hooray for Hollywood—unless you're a conservative." The Hill, March 15, 2020. https://thehill.com/opinion/technology/487640-hooray-for-hollywood-unless-youre-a-conservative

19. Ibid.

20. Kurtz, Howard. "Blacklist? Hollywood liberals backtrack after seeking list of Trump donors," Fox News, September 5, 2019. https://www.foxnews.com/media/blacklist-hollywood-liberals-backtrack-after-seeking-list-of-trump-donors

21. Ibid.

22. Morini, Marco. "Same-sex marriage and other moral taboos: Cultural acceptances, change in American public opinion and the evidence from the opinion polls," *European Journal of American Studies* 11 (2017): 1–21. https://doi.org/10.4000/ejas.11824

23. Read, Glenna L., van Driel, Irene I., and Potter, Robert F. "Same-sex couples in advertisements: An investigation of the role of implicit attitudes on cognitive processing and evaluation," *Journal of Advertising* 47 (2018): 182–97.

24. Cohen, Sascha. "How one movie changed LGBT history," *Time*, March 17, 2015. https://time.com/3742951/boys-in-the-band/

25. Ibid.

26. "Cruising," IMDB, 1980. https://www.imdb.com/title/tt0080569/plotsummary

27. "Desert Hearts," IMDB, 1985. https://www.imdb.com/title/tt0089015/plotsummary

28. "The Celluloid Closet," IMDB, 1995. https://www.imdb.com/title/tt0112651/plotsummary

29. "Bound," IMDB, 1996. https://www.imdb.com/title/tt0115736/plotsummary

30. "Boys Don't Cry," IMDB, 1999. https://www.imdb.com/title/tt0171804/plotsummary

31. "Angels in America," IMDB, 2003. https://www.imdb.com/title/tt0318997/plotsummary

32. "Brokeback Mountain," IMDB, 2005. https://www.imdb.com/title/tt0388795/plotsummary

33. "Carol," IMDB, 2015. https://www.imdb.com/title/tt2402927/plotsummary

34. "Beat per Minute," IMDB, 2017. https://www.imdb.com/title/tt6135348/plotsummary

35. "Call Me by Your Name," IMDB, 2017. https://www.imdb.com/title/tt5726616/plotsummary

36. "Growing support for gay marriage: Changed minds and changing demographics," Pew Research Center, March 20, 2013. https://www.pewresearch.org/politics/2013/03/20/growing-support-for-gay-marriage-changed-minds-and-changing-demographics/; *Morning Edition.* "Hidden Brain: America's changing attitudes toward gay people," NPR, April 17, 2019. https://www.npr.org/2019/04/17/714212984/hidden-brain-americas-changing-attitudes-toward-gay-people

37. McCarthy, Justin. "Record-high 70% in U.S. support same-sex marriage," Gallup, June 8, 2021. https://news.gallup.com/poll/350486/record-high-support-same-sex-marriage.aspx

38. "Attitudes on same-sex marriage," PEW Research Center, May 14, 2020. https://www.pewforum.org/fact-sheet/changing-attitudes-on-gay-marriage/

39. "Stances of faiths on LGBTQ issues: Alliance of Baptists," Human Rights Campaign, accessed January 9, 2022. https://www.hrc.org/resources/stances-of-faiths-on-lgbt-issues-alliance-of-baptists

40. Polling and Analysis. "Religious groups' official positions on same-sex marriage," PEW Research Center, December 7, 2012. https://www.pewforum.org/2012/12/07/religious-groups-official-positions-on-same-sex-marriage/

41. Ibid.

42. Paulsen, David. "Episcopalians rally support for LGBTQ community after Vatican refuses same-sex blessings," Episcopal News Service, March 17, 2021. https://www.episcopalnewsservice.org/2021/03/17/episcopalians-rally-support-for-lgbtq-community-after-vatican-refuses-same-sex-blessings/

43. "Stances of faiths on LGBTQ issues: Presbyterian Church (USA)," Human Rights Campaign. https://www.hrc.org/resources/stances-of-faiths-on-lgbt-issues-presbyterian-church-usa

44. Polling and Analysis. "Religious groups' official positions,"

45. "What is the Church's position on homosexuality?" The People of the United Methodist Church. https://www.umc.org/en/content/ask-the-umc-what-is-the-churchs-position-on-homosexuality

46. Polling and Analysis. "Religious groups' official positions."

47. Vance, Laura. "Rejecting women's ordination: The 60th General Conference Session of the Seventh-Day Adventist World Church," *Nova Religio: The Journal of Alternative and Emergent Religions* 21, no. 1 (2017): 85–99. https://www.jstor.org/stable/26417758.

48. Ibid.

49. Ibid.

50. "Female Priests? Never, says Pope Francis," Universal Life Church, November 4, 2016. https://www.themonastery.org/blog/female-priests-never-says-pope-francis

51. Vance. "Rejecting women's ordination."

52. "Seventh-day Adventist World Church Statistics 2020," Seventh-Day Adventist Church, January 4, 2021. https://www.adventist.org/statistics/seventh-day-adventist-world-church-statistics-2020/; Vance. "Rejecting women's ordination."

53. Vance. "Rejecting women's ordination."

54. Adventist Church Twitter Post, December 18, 2021, 3:53 PM PST. https://twitter.com/adventistchurch/status/1472354434776719362?s=20

55. Vance. "Rejecting women's ordination."

56. Ibid.

57. Ibid.

58. "Dr. Jan Paulsen—The San Antonio Address," Equal Ordination, July 30, 2015. https://www.youtube.com/watch?v=oWwSAaF5ZV8

59. Vance. "Rejecting women's ordination."

60. Newton, Jim. "Opinion: Pasadena's anti-evolution, anti-gay health director has some explaining to do," *Los Angeles Times*, May 2, 2014. https://www.latimes.com/opinion/opinion-la/la-ol-eric-walsh-pasadena-health-department-20140502-story.html#navtype=outfit

61. Walsh, Eric. "The prescription for a healthy city," YouTube, May 28, 2012. https://www.youtube.com/watch?v=EtUz4g37yQw

62. Gazzar, Brenda. "Pasadena health director cites Mother Teresa in remarks to annual prayer breakfast," *Pasadena Star-News*, May 3, 2012. https://www.pasadenastarnews.com/2012/05/03/pasadena-health-director-cites-mother-teresa-in-remarks-to-annual-prayer-breakfast/

63. Ibid.

64. Sahlin, Monte. "Controversy raised around Pasadena official for his Adventist Sermons," *Pasadena Star-News*, May 6, 2014. https://atoday.org/controversy-raised-around-pasadena-official-for-his-adventist-sermons/; Walsh, Eric. "Dr. Eric Walsh—My testimony | Tribulation's Song," YouTube, July 15, 2019. https://www.youtube.com/watch?v=ud61qHfaGpg

65. Shyong, Frank. "Pasadena health director put on leave over controversial comments," *Los Angeles Times*, May 1, 2014. https://www.latimes.com/local/la-me-pasadena-leave-20140502-story.html

66. Abcarian, Robin. "Pasadena City College's commencement speaker fiasco re-ignites," *Los Angeles Times*, April 29, 2014. https://www.latimes.com/local/abcarian/la-me-ra-pasadena-college-commencement-speaker-fiasco-20140429-story.html

67. Ibid.

68. Girardot, Frank C. "Dr. Eric Walsh's beliefs disqualify him from being head of Public Health Department," *Pasadena Star-News*, April 30, 2014. https://www.pasadenastarnews.com/2014/04/30/dr-eric-walshs-beliefs-disqualify-him-from-being-head-of-public-health-department/

69. Gold, Lauren. "Pasadena health director Dr. Eric Walsh sermons, city reaction cause Twitter storm," *Pasadena Star-News*, May 2, 2014. https://www.pasadenastarnews.com/2014/05/02/pasadena-health-director-dr-eric-walsh-sermons-city-reaction-cause-twitter-storm/

70. Gold, Lauren. "Pasadena public health director Dr. Eric Walsh placed on administrative leave after homophobic sermon furor," *Pasadena Star-News*, May 1, 2014. https://www.pasadenastarnews.com/2014/05/01/pasadena-public-health-director-dr-eric-walsh-placed-on-administrative-leave-after-homophobic-sermon-furor/; Shyong, "Pasadena health director put on leave."

71. Harris, Gerald. "The devil came down to Georgia and stole sermons," The Christian Index, October 26, 2016. https://christianindex.org/stories/the-devil-came-down-to-georgia-and-stole-sermons,1053

72. Ibid.

73. First Liberty Institute. "Georgia pays almost a quarter of a million dollars to end pastor's lawsuit," First Liberty—Press Release, February 6, 2017. https://firstliberty.org/media/georgia-pays-almost-a-quarter-of-a-million-dollars-to-end-pastors-lawsuit/

74. Gold, Lauren. "Seventh-day Adventist Church: Pasadena Public Health Director Dr. Eric Walsh does not represent church," *Pasadena Star-News*, May 6, 2014. https://www.pasadenastarnews.com/2014/05/06/seventh-day-adventist-church-pasadena-public-health-director-dr-eric-walsh-does-not-represent-church/

75. Walsh, Eric. "Dr. Eric Walsh—My Testimony | Tribulation's Song"

76. "Official Beliefs of the Seventh-day Adventist Church," Seventh-day Adventists Church. https://www.adventist.org/beliefs/

77. Ibid.

Chapter 5

Media Influence in Schools

Giving the 1980 valedictory address at the University of Dallas, Gary D. Cieslak wrestled with the concept of "ideas." What are ideas? What do they do and what is their place in the advancement of the society? In the speech, he points out that education does not constitute of merely taking notes or memorizing quotes. It also involves taking in ideas, analyzing them, and accepting whatever truth is in them.

"We may not always agree with them but our common predicament here on this planet gives us the responsibility to listen to what the world is saying,"[1] Cieslak said. In Gary Cieslak's generation, education involved listening to different ideas and engaging in earnest debate in pursuit of the truth. College campuses were places where ideas flourished. Some were brilliant ideas, others fantastical, and yet others stupid. But people listened to them all.

That was nearly half a century ago. Today the American campus has radically changed. More and more, speech is being policed with many speakers, especially conservatives, being prevented from speaking on campus. Grand Canyon University declined to allow conservative commentator Ben Shapiro for fear that his presence was too "divisive and run counter to the school's mission."[2] In other words, the school was afraid of possible violence because those who did not subscribe to Shapiro's point of view would be aggravated.

Shapiro also had his invitation to speak at the University of California at Los Angeles (UCLA) revoked because the university considered his speech not a debate but an attack. He was scheduled to talk about microaggressions, Black Lives Matter, and safe spaces.[3] He was later allowed to visit the campus after the school was threatened with legal action.[4]

In 2016, Business Insider compiled a list of individuals who had been disinvited on campuses.[5] The list is very long. It includes Janet Mock, Nicholas Dirks, Anita Alvarez, Bassem Eid, Action Bronson, Emily Wong, John Brennan, Nir Karkat, Jason Riley, John Derbyshire, and Suzanne Venker. Janet Mock's speech on Brown University was shut down because students "believed that it was better for Mock not to speak at all than to do so at an event connected to the Hillel chapter for the Ivy League college and the Rhode Island School of Design."[6]

Intolerance on school campuses is not only directed at people from outside the campus. A political culture has now been created on the campus in which only certain groups of people can be victims, even when they are aggressors. In other words, other groups of people have been canceled, perpetually regarded as aggressors, and their viewpoint not worthy of being listened to.

In August 2020, Rose Ritch, a Jewish undergraduate at the University of Southern California (USC) resigned under pressure as vice president of the Undergraduate Student Government (USG) following a campaign that featured denunciations of her support for Israel, including some with anti-Semitic overtones.[7] Ritch was subjected to vicious online harassment, and her qualification to hold elected office was questioned on the basis of her professed Zionism. Her accusers associated her professed Zionism with inflammatory accusations of racism, colonialism, and white supremacy.[8] Her resignation prompted a furor, which eventually led to the university president's condemnation of the harassment.

According to the *Los Angeles Times*, "Rose Ritch, a San Francisco native, came to USC to study dance but soon widened her academic interests to sociology, law, history, and culture. Socially, too, she thrived: winning election as student body vice president in February, nurturing her strong Jewish identity through the Hillel organization and Trojans for Israel."[9] During her campaign to run for vice president of the USG, Ritch was subjected to brutal harassment by some students on the campus. She was consistently called a "Pro-Israel White Supremacist." Her campaign posters were frequently taken down.

Some students even questioned her qualification to lead the student body given her previous leadership of a pro-Israel group on the campus. These students somehow believed that she would not support them when it came to questions of boycotting Israel. They did not feel her loyalty would be with USC.

Ritch went on to win that election.

The issue became worse after the death of George Floyd on June 1, 2020. The president of USG was accused of insensitive remarks and "micro aggression" after he had allegedly said that having a Jewish student on his team made it diverse, a comment that did not sit well with some black students and others. Ritch was the vice president of the USG.

The social media campaign @black_at_usc began, and it had started as a way for black students and other students of color to voice discontent about their treatment at USC. Soon, many anonymously posted accusations were made. On June 26, 2020, one student created a petition asking the president of the USG to resign because of "'recent uncoverings of racial misconduct,' based on the postings on the @black_at_usc account."[10]

Even though Ritch was not mentioned in this petition, many ugly comments attacking her were made in response to the petition and on many other platforms. The Alliance for Academic Freedom details some of those horrible comments as follows:

> "'Him and the Zionist need to be IMPEACHED'; 'Tell your Zionist ass VP to resign too'; 'The president is trash and so is the VP who is a proud Zionist'; 'Would you like to share that not only is Rose a Zionist who indoctrinated the rest of USG to be Zionists, she is also an above-the-waist-only bisexual'; 'warms my heart to see all the Zionists from USC and USG getting relentlessly cyberbullied.'"[11]

When the USG president eventually resigned, Ritch was in line to succeed him. Unfortunately, the student started attacking her, too, because she had not endorsed attacks on the former president. The student said, "Her silence aids and abets the already taxing oppression and microaggressions that Black students face at USC daily."[12]

The students then staged an impeachment hearing for Ritch. However, university administrators postponed the hearing after the Louis D. Brandeis Center wrote a letter detailing the systematic harassment Ritch had faced. In its letter, the Louis D. Brandeis Center demanded that the USC administrators "immediately halt the impeachment proceedings against Ms. Ritch which are unquestionably and deeply rooted in Jew hatred and unlawfully deny her an equal opportunity to participate in USC campus life."[13]

The attacks on Ritch continued, and when she could not withstand them anymore, she resigned. In her resignation letter, Ritch stated:

> We all have the right to our opinions, and to disagree. But in today's day and age, our campuses have shifted from authentic, in-person conversations to comments and retweets, and we "cancel" anyone with whom we disagree on any issue. There is a disturbing lack of nuance or willingness to grapple with the messy complexities of an issue, and there is no longer any room for change or growth.
>
> Students made presumptions about my Zionist identity and leapt to unfair conclusions. No one asked me to explain my passion for Israel. No one asked to learn together, to try to understand and build connections. Instead, the people with whom I have shared a campus with for years, the people whom I desperately want to serve, have tried to make me feel ashamed, invalidated, and dehumanized because of who I am.[14]

Outraged by the harassment Ritch faced, a group of USC faculty—comprising prominent members of national and international academies; educators and researchers in medicine, science, humanities, the arts and communication;

and champions of human rights and free speech—signed an open letter calling on the USC campus to reject intolerance and hatred that led to Ritch's resignation.[15]

The letter described Ritch's harassment as "blatant discrimination on the basis of a student's belief, identity, or national origin." The letter stated:

> We reject in the strongest possible terms any and all attempts to associate Zionism with such inflammatory accusations as racism, colonialism, and white supremacy, which are diametrically antithetical to Zionist ideas and aims. We are appalled that such characterizations of Zionism were the basis for calls for Rose Ritch's resignation and continue to be voiced by certain organizations on this campus.
>
> As supporters of the Zionist idea—the right of the Jewish people to a homeland and self-determination—we stand by the rights of all people, including Israelis and Palestinians, to freedom, dignity, and peaceful coexistence, and to advocate for their causes with fairness and respect on our campus and in the world.

The Alliance for Academic Freedom also condemned the harassment saying:

> Academic freedom protects the right of qualified faculty and students to run for or be appointed to campus offices. Campaigns to discredit those candidates or officers based in attacks on their race, religion, gender, sexuality, ethnicity, or national origin undermine that right and must be rejected unequivocally. So, too, should attacks on an individual based on political litmus tests—including one's views about Israel or Zionism.[16]

The Alliance for Academic Freedom also faulted the administration for failing to forcefully speak out on the issue early. On her part, USC president Carol L. Folt issued a statement of support for Ritch and condemned "anti-Semitic attacks on her character and the online harassment." She also announced a new university-wide initiative to counter hate with tangible action.

The role of the media in fomenting these examples of campus intolerance was seen in how the *Los Angeles Times* covered the story. In an article titled "At USC, 2 Determined Women Spoke Out. Ugly Attacks over Racism, Anti-Semitism, Zionism Took Over," the author Teresa Watanabe puts Ritch on the same moral ground as the person who was partly responsible for organizing the unfair campaign to impeach her, Abeer Tijani, presumably because Tijani is a woman of color.[17]

Even though it is clear from the story that Ritch was the victim in this whole incident, the *Los Angeles Times* story portrays Tijani as also a victim, because when people condemned the attacks against Ritch, rightly describing them as anti-Semitic attacks, Tijani felt victimized. As far as the media is concerned, certain segments of society have an absolute right to claim victim-hood regardless of the level of harassment they inflict on others. The manner in which the story of Ritch and Tijani was told in the press is emblematic of the way the media has helped to create a culture of victimhood on university campuses.

The university administration, itself, cannot escape blame. The problem with the University of Southern California, and all universities across the country, is that this intolerance on campus is being enabled when university leadership, on social media, sometimes post messages that appear to support activities, riots, or demonstrations of some far-left intolerance groups. Whether they are doing it to appease the vocal intolerant far-left groups for fear that they may be accused of being silent and become targets, or not, university presidents are increasingly using their social media to add their voices to complex divisive cultural issues. Unfortunately, some intolerant groups on campus take these statements as an endorsement.

For USC, the issue of Rose Ritch was not to be the last one. It was quickly followed by another similarly intolerant incident. Another student posted online incendiary statements directed at the Jewish people. These included statements like, "I want to kill every motherf**cking Zionist"; "Death to Israel and its b**tch the U.S."; "Israel has no history just a criminal record"; "yel3an el yahood (curse the Jews)."[18]

Once again, concerned faculty wrote a letter to USC president Carol L. Folt, expressing their dismay at the level of open expressions of anti-Semitism and Zionophobia within the campus, and of the silence of the university leadership which amounted to tacit acceptance of a toxic atmosphere of hatred and hostility.[19]

For her part, the student, just like the student in the previous incident, considered herself a victim. When asked if in retrospect she would have done anything differently, the student responded, "I just really wish I didn't have to think about what I would change. I wish people didn't expect Palestinians to be the perfect victims."[20]

University campuses have also become very political. Instead of providing freedoms to all, universes are now putting emphasis on giving other groups more freedoms because of their history. For example, universities are now creating what are known as "comfort zones" for minorities and underrepresented people. Apart from the obvious unequal treatment of students, these practices also send a wrong message to minorities and underrepresented groups. By shielding these students from alternative ideas and philosophies, universities are equipping them poorly for real life.

Manny Nelson, a rising junior at the time, wrote in *Forbes* in support of the need for black and brown students to have safe spaces on campus. Apparently, "safe spaces on campus" are places on campus created solely for the ownership or patronage of black and brown students. Manny writes, "From having to constantly interact with privileged white students to debating faculty on the appropriateness of their lessons, I was in need of a space where I could just be myself and not have to defend my existence or right to be there."[21]

The problem with these safe spaces is that they give the students an erroneous perception that the only obstacle affecting the advancement of any student is race. So, if you are black, you have an obstacle in your path; and if you are white, you have no obstacle in your path. The reality of life is that there are many, many obstacles in a person's life trying to hold him or her back. That is true for all races. Yes, for black and brown students, one of those obstacles is race. White people may not have to deal with that so much. Yet they still have to deal with all the other obstacles as well. Everybody has to deal with a myriad of obstacles.

Even white people have to deal with uniquely white problems, such as being on the negative end of affirmative action. Some of those problems may not be as grave as those black people face, but in the grand scheme of things when one considers the many problems each has to face, just focusing on race is a big disservice to minorities. To prepare for life, a person must be trained to handle all problems regardless of whether they are race based or not. By creating a culture-of-victimhood mentality, the universities are equipping minorities poorly for life and, in the process, unfortunately perpetrating stereotypes.

Some of the things happening in schools are so unbelievable, one wonders whether scholars are still in charge of academia. In some schools, they have started fighting what they call "whiteness," in order to make the communities safe for everybody.[22] Signs of this toxic "whiteness" are said to include individualism, worship of the written word, and objectivity. Apparently, these are trends white people must fight in themselves in order to make themselves acceptable in society.

Incidentally, those same qualities also happen to be traits that one needs in order to succeed in life—individual thought, a value of education, and objectivity. And so, by assigning these to white people only, the schools are indirectly saying that only white people are naturally equipped to succeed. The schools end up reinforcing the message they wanted to destroy.

It is not wrong for schools to discuss race. They cannot discuss it enough. What is wrong is to demonize some groups of people with the hope that they will make other groups of people feel better. For instance, some races are being made to feel bad just because their ancestors won a war many years ago, while those people whose ancestors lost wars are being made to feel good as if they are owed gratitude by society, or as if there is honor in losing. Pioneering, inventing, and war victory should not make anybody feel bad about themselves or their heritage. Modern civilization thrives on competition. Society must never judge yesterday using today's standards.

There is no question that a media hand is behind this wave of victimhood mentality sweeping across university campuses, and beyond. The two incidents at USC were not covered wall to wall by the media. In fact, when they were covered, as was the case with the *Los Angeles Times*, the aggressor and the victim were almost put on the same moral ground.

Imagine for a while if, in the first USC incident, the tables were turned, and it was Rose Ritch (the Jewish girl) who was the orchestrating a campaign against Abeer Tijani (the black girl). Such a story would have been covered wall to wall by CNN, MSNBC, and all the other news networks. Just as in the recent case of Jussie Smollett, the media would not even have waited for more information before blasting the alleged perpetrator.

Although it did not happen on a campus, the case of Jussie Smollett illustrates how the media get oxygen out of these victimhood-mentality issues. Smollett, a famous actor on the popular television show *Empire*, had arranged a fake racist and homophobic attack on himself in Chicago in 2019. He had reported to the police that the attackers had shouted "MAGA country," a reference to the Donald Trump campaign slogan "Make America Great Again," which some liberals describe as racist. He also had a noose around his neck— a racist symbol harking back to the dark days of segregation in America.

The issue was suspect from the beginning, but the media did not care. The story was covered wall to wall and portrayed as evidence that America is a dangerous place for minorities and people of color. TV anchors of color, themselves highly protected and well-paid millionaires, went on air and described how they are victims in America. After a short period of police investigation, Jussie himself was charged with reporting a false incident to the police. He had deliberately staged the racist and homophobic crime to bring attention to himself, a black and gay person.

On campus and elsewhere, this behavior is being enabled by the media, which encourages certain segments of the population to look at themselves as victims, regardless of their social status in society. Part of the problem is also that universities have been investing a lot of money to make sure that their campuses are politically correct. Thus, the "political correctness" philosophy has been entrenched on the campus.

Dr. Mark J. Perry is professor emeritus at the University of Michigan. On December 30, 2018, he tweeted that the University of Michigan had at least eighty-two full-time diversity officers on its staff. The annual payroll cost to cover those eighty-two diversity officers was $10.6 million. This amount of money was equivalent to the amount of funding needed to support full in-state tuition for 708 students![23]

Amid the victimhood mentality and intolerance on college campuses today, it is the quality of education that is the real casualty. In academia, professors have long been chosen and promoted based on their ability to publish their ideas and research results in peer-reviewed journals. The journal peer-review process is supposed to be rigorous. When a paper is submitted to the journal for publication, the editor is supposed to first send it to experts in the field to review its merit. These experts normally suggest revisions before recommending the paper for publication. Most papers get rejected.

This rigorous process has long been used to as a selective process for professors. Good professors working on interesting, important research will have their papers accepted for publication in prestigious journals. Unfortunately, when the peer-review system became corrupted with political correctness, the professors chosen based on this system are compromised, leading to compromised education as well.

Peter Boghossian has long been a critic of postmodern ideology in the academy. Until recently, he was an untenured assistant professor of philosophy at Portland State University (PSU).[24] Boghossian and his colleagues argued that critical studies scholars tend to validate anything as long as it is aligned with their politics. To prove their point, Boghossian and his colleagues published twenty fake papers on such ridiculous topics as "canine rape culture in dog parks" to "fat bodybuilding" and "adaption of Mein Kampf."[25]

The intention was to show how much the academic world has been corrupted with political correctness and shallowness. Indeed, of those twenty fake papers, seven were accepted by journals. The accepted papers had politically correct jargon in them. One was on "queer performativity in urban dog parks" and another on "imperialist astronomy."[26]

The question as to whether the quality of education on campuses is being affected by the political correctness culture now permeating them is not an unreasonable one. This is even being reflected in the type of valedictorian speeches that are being given today. The older speeches were more concerned with great and eternal things. Gary Cieslak's valedictory speech, above, talked about ideas and how they can help graduates improve society. More recent valedictorian speeches from different universities across the country seem to center around political correctness and victimhood mentality, and the lack of intellectuality is evident.

The politicization of the campus, the policing of free speech on campus, and the victimhood culture being nurtured are all being influenced by the powerful press that seeks to control every aspect of citizens' lives through political correctness. The media has become too powerful for this civilization.

The best and only hope for humankind is a well-educated citizenry capable of standing up in defense of freedom of speech, holding the media accountable every time it crosses the line. Unfortunately, this goal will not be achieved unless the students are trained to value freedom of thought on the college campus.

It is therefore imperative to make schools laboratories of democracy by opening them up to speeches of different kinds and sensitizing the students to different points of view. As Gary Cieslak said in his valedictorian speech, "We may not always agree with them [opposing ideas] but our common predicament here on this planet gives us the responsibility to listen to what the world is saying."

NOTES

1. Cieslak, Gary D., "Valedictory Address: Gary D. Cieslak" (1980), Valedictorian Speeches, 23. https://digitalcommons.udallas.edu/valedictorian-speeches/23

2. Nakamoto-White, Ellie. "GCU stirs outcry after preventing right-wing commentator's speech," AZ Central, February 2, 2019, 4:15 PM MT. https://www.azcentral.com/story/news/local/phoenix/2019/02/01/gcu-stirs-outcry-after-preventing-right-wing-commentator-ben-shapiro-speech/2749067002/

3. Jackson, Abby. "'Disinvitations' for college speakers are on the rise—here's a list of people turned away this year," Business Insider, July 28, 2016. https://www.businessinsider.com/list-of-disinvited-speakers-at-colleges-2016-7

4. Ibid.

5. Ibid.

6. Shire, Emily. "Brown students shut down trans activist's speech—because Israel," Daily Beast, April 13, 2017, 4:32 PM EST. https://www.thedailybeast.com/brown-students-shut-down-trans-activists-speechbecause-israel

7. Alliance for Academic Freedom. "Are you now or have you ever been a Zionist?" The Third Narrative, August 24, 2020. https://thirdnarrative.org/anti-zionism-antisemitism/are-you-now-or-have-you-ever-been-a-zionist/

8. "An Open letter to the USC community on supporting Zionist students at USC," August 30, 2020. https://usc-faaz.org

9. Watanabe, Teresa. "At USC, 2 determined women spoke out. Ugly attacks over racism, anti-Semitism, Zionism took over," *Los Angeles Times*, October 18, 2020. https://www.latimes.com/california/story/2020-10-18/social-media-attacks-usc-free-speech-debate-racism

10. Alliance for Academic Freedom. "Are you now?"

11. Alliance for Academic Freedom. "Are you now?"

12. Alliance for Academic Freedom. "Are you now?"

13. Lewin, Alyza D. "Letter to the USC president," The Louis D. Brandeis Center, July 7, 2020. https://jewishinsider.com/wp-content/uploads/2020/08/Letter-to-President-Folt-and-VP-Crisp-July-7-2020.pdf

14. Lange, David. "USG vice president Rose Ritch resigns over antisemitic attacks because she is a Zionist," Israellycool, August 6, 2020. https://www.israellycool.com

/2020/08/06/usg-vice-president-rose-ritch-resigns-over-antisemitic-attacks-because
-she-is-a-zionist/

15. Krylov, Ann, and Warshel, Arieh. "Letter to the editor: Following Rose Ritch resignation, USC's climate of inclusion must be redefined to include Zionism," *Daily Trojan*, October 2, 2020. https://dailytrojan.com/2020/10/02/letter-to-the-editor
-following-rose-ritch-resignation-uscs-climate-of-inclusion-must-be-redefined-to
-include-zionism/

16. Alliance for Academic Freedom. "Are you now?"

17. Watanabe. "At USC, 2 determined women spoke out."

18. "An open letter to the leadership of USC," December 1, 2021. https://usc-faaz
-12-2021.org/

19. Ibid.

20. Gerber, Marisa. "'Toxic atmosphere of hatred.' USC faculty outraged over response to student's tweets," *Los Angeles Times*, December 14, 2021. https://www
.latimes.com/california/story/2021-12-14/usc-faculty-open-letter-student-tweets

21. Nelson, Manny. "Black and Brown students are in need of safe spaces on campus!" *Forbes*, August 11, 2021, 9:00 AM EDT. https://www.forbes.com/sites
/civicnation/2021/08/11/black-and-brown-students-are-in-need-of-safe-spaces-on
-campus/?sh=2be9dfa06000

22. Powell, Michael. "New York's private schools tackle white privilege. It has not been easy," *New York Times*, April 27, 2021. https://www.nytimes.com/2021/08/27/
us/new-york-private-schools-racism.html

23. Perry, Mark J. Twitter Post, December 30, 2018, 6:28 PM PST. https://twitter
.com/Mark_J_Perry/status/1079564863435870208?s=20; "Dr. Mark J. Perry," Mackinac Center for Public Policy. https://www.mackinac.org/about/board-of-scholars/173

24. "A professor's resignation highlights pressures within academia to conform," *Economist*, September 25, 2021. https://www.economist.com/united-states/2021/09
/25/a-professors-resignation-highlights-pressures-within-academia-to-conform

25. Flaherty, Colleen. "Blowback against a hoax," *Inside Higher Ed*, January 8, 2019. https://www.insidehighered.com/news/2019/01/08/author-recent-academic
-hoax-faces-disciplinary-action-portland-state

26. Ibid.; "A professor's resignation."

Chapter 6

Hypocrisy of the Social Media Platforms

The preface of this book talks about the American "Towel of Babel," an allegory signifying a puzzling development in America, where the very principles on which the United States of America was built are now under attack. Nowhere is this development more evident than in Silicon Valley among the social media platforms. The social media platforms, as known today, would not have existed if it was not for Section 230 of the Communications Decency Act, a law passed by Congress in 1996.

Section 230 protects websites from being legally responsible for what users post on their sites. That means an "interactive computer service" cannot be held responsible for what third parties publish or say on the platform.[1] According to the Verge, Sen. Ron Wyden (D-OR) and Rep. Chris Cox (R-CA) had crafted Section 230 to give website owners freedom to develop and moderate websites without having to worry about legal liability.[2] Facebook, Twitter, Google, and many media sites would not have existed without this Section 230.

Some people have argued that, given that most people's lives are affected by the internet, Section 230 gives too much power to unelected people, and in some cases non-Americans, to make important decisions to control and sometimes censor the general public. Even though social media platforms and big tech have been highly favored in this manner, it appears they harbor some sort of animosity toward the United States. They have always reserved their wrath for the United States. More citizens and leaders of the United States constantly face harassment, discrimination, and, in some cases, ultimately bans than citizens of other countries.

Speaking to *Newsweek*, Shagun Jhaver, a postdoctoral scholar in the Paul G. Allen School of Computer Science & Engineering at the University of Washington and an affiliate of the Berkman Klein Center for Internet & Society at Harvard University, said that his research shows that that Twitter's use of warning labels had been very "US-centric," in that most users with labels tended to be Americans.[3] "My hope is Twitter will use such labeling to counter misinformation across a wider range of issues and countries," *Newsweek* quotes Jhaver.[4]

The *Washington Post* reported that two days after the January 6 riots on the US Capitol, Vijaya Gadde, Twitter's senior policy executive, addressed the company's 5,200 employees via video imploring them to be patient while her team decided what to do with President Trump's Twitter account.[5] Gadde's team later decided to ban Trump permanently from the social network. By the time Trump was banned from the social network, he already had had a number of run-ins with the social media giant. Trump accused social networks of being against him and conservatives generally.

At times, it appeared as if Trump was right. His tweets were constantly labeled as false or misleading while corresponding hyperbole by his critics did not meet the same scrutiny by the social network giant. Ironically, Twitter was formed to be a marketplace of ideas where different views would be exchanged and debated. Now here they were banning the leader of the United States, who represented millions of citizens. The *Washington Post* reported that apart from Twitter, Trump and his supporters were also banned from Facebook, Twitch, Snap, Spotify, and other services.[6] The main reason for the ban was the claim that the 2020 election was rigged and stolen.

The banning of Trump from social media sent a chilling message around the world, starting from Jack Dorsey himself, who is the cofounder and then-CEO of Twitter. Dorsey felt that "the suspension reflected a failure on his company's part to maintain a space for civil discourse."[7] German chancellor Angela Merkel was very troubled by the decision. Through her spokesman she said, "The right to freedom of opinion is of fundamental importance."[8] She called the decision problematic in that the president's accounts were permanently suspended.[9] Merkel believed that elected officials, not private companies, should decide speech limitations.[10]

Merkel's statement makes one wonder loudly; of those employees who were impatiently and angrily pushing Vijaya Gadde to suspend Trump's account, how many of them were Americans? How about Gadde's committee that decided to ban Trump, how many of the voting members were Americans?

These are fair questions. Twitter moderates a conversation marketplace for all Americans. Twitter has become so big and so important that to fully participate in the American conversation, one must be on the platform. And when a decision has to be made to take a person who represents a significant fraction of Americans off the platform, the instrument that makes such a decision must be vetted carefully.

In fact, some—not all—of those people angrily or silently demanding that their employers take certain positions in American politics, are themselves not Americans. The laws of the United States allow companies to hire foreign workers easily through H1B visa programs. Thus, lots of non-Americans are allowed to come to the United States and work in the social media industry that has a big impact on American lives. The paradox of America is that it has become more prosperous and famous so that most people in the world want to come to America. Yet the moment they arrive in America, they immediately start to try and change it to be exactly like the country they are fleeing from.

Through it all, Twitter insisted that they banned Trump because they were just following their rules. A lot of people, however, noticed the hypocrisy. Immediately after the permanent ban of Trump from Twitter, Ajit Pai, the then-chairman of the US Federal Communications Commission shared on Twitter screenshots of some of very incendiary tweets the Ayatollah Ali Khamenei of Iran had sent out.[11] Pai challenged Twitter to explain why these tweets were still online while Trump had been banned.

The Ayatollah tweets included such strong words as:

The Zionist regime is a deadly, cancerous growth and a detriment to this region. It will undoubtedly be uprooted and destroyed. Then, the shame will fall on those who put their facilities at the service of normalization of relations with this regime.[12]

The elimination of the Zionist regime does not mean the massacre of the Jewish ppl. The ppl of Palestine should hold a referendum. Any political sys they vote for should govern in all of Palestine. The only remedy until the removal of the Zionist regime is firm, armed resistance.[13]

The struggle to free #Palestine is #Jihad in the way of God. Victory in such a struggle has been guaranteed, because the person, even if killed, will receive 'one of the two excellent things.' Also, crimes against Palestine trouble any human's conscience & inspire opposition.[14]

We will support and assist any nation or any group anywhere who opposes and fights the Zionist regime, and we do not hesitate to say this. #FlyTheFlag[15]

The Twitter account @Khamenei_IR, although not verified by Twitter, is widely believed to be owned by Ayatollah Ali Khamenei and regularly posts incendiary messages.

Among those puzzled by Twitter's apparent double standard was Jason Brodsky, policy director of US advocacy group United Against Nuclear Iran. In a statement to VOA Persia, Brodsky said, "Twitter accounts of Khamenei, other autocrats and their representatives include deeply hateful and dangerous content that incites violence against groups. We've seen Khamenei's call for the elimination of Israel, which is incitement. So if Twitter has a policy against incitement of violence, it needs to be applied uniformly."[16]

Later, in early 2021, Twitter did ban another of Khamenei's accounts, @khamenei_site, after it posted a video of a drone flying at Donald Trump.[17] In early 2022, another account, @KhameneiSite, was permanently banned after it posted a video depicting the assassination of Donald Trump.[18] However, as Twitter itself and the *Jerusalem Post* mentioned, the banned accounts are not the main accounts of Ayatollah Ali Khamenei. As of January 18, 2022, those main accounts of the Ayatollah were still active.[19]

Twitter has also overlooked several irresponsible tweets from the Chinese government. Zhao Lijian, a Chinese foreign ministry spokesman has been making waves for being very aggressive on Twitter. Among his outrageous tweets was one in which he accused the Australian army of murdering Afghani children. He attached to the tweet an illustration of an Australian soldier about to slit the throat of an Afghan child.[20] The tweet sent shock waves through Australia.

On the US side, Zhao is most famous for a tweet that claimed that the coronavirus did not start in China but in the United States. He claimed that it was US soldiers who brought the virus to Wuhan.[21] As of January 18, 2022, Zhao's account is still active on Twitter.

Twitter's apparent double standard did not stop with selective banning of world leaders. In the run-up to the 2020 presidential elections, the *New York Post* published a story claiming that "Hunter Biden's abandoned laptop carried proof he sold influence while his father served as vice president."[22] Twitter said they were banning the article due to questions about "the origins of the materials." The company said that their policy prohibited direct distribution of private material obtained through hacking.[23] Another tech giant, Facebook, also restricted the story. Facebook claimed that there were questions about its validity. A Facebook spokesperson said that restricting the article was part of their standard process to reduce the spread of misinformation.[24]

Surprisingly, however, when the *New York Times* illegally obtained Donald Trump's tax documents, which the *Times* said contained information "extending over more than two decades, revealing struggling properties, vast write-offs, an audit battle and hundreds of millions in debt coming due," neither Twitter nor Facebook banned the article or restricted it from being disseminated.[25] The story was distributed on Facebook, Twitter, and many other social networks.

On April 25, 2022, billionaire Elon Musk acquired Twitter for $44 billion. Musk cited his desire to protect free speech as his motivation for buying the social network platform. In a statement on Twitter on April 26, Musk defined the free speech he envisioned for Twitter as "that which matches the law."

If people want less free speech, he said, they should ask the government to pass laws to that effect. He claimed to be "against censorship that goes far beyond the law."

Another tech giant that has demonstrated an inexplicable hypocrisy is Google. In 2018 Google announced that it would no longer work with the US Defense Department on a contract to provide artificial intelligence (AI) for analyzing drone footage.[26] Google put this decision down to "ethics." Its new ethics guideline would not allow it to work with the Defense Department on such issues, the company said.[27]

The truth is that Google had faced backslash among its employees for working with the Defense Department on this project. Yet, when Google went ahead and set up an artificial intelligence lab in China, there was no backlash from the same employees. Apparently, the Google employees who had protested working with the Defense Department, saw no ethical issues with the Chinese military.

Peter Thiel, a famous Silicon Valley investor, pointed out this Google double standard in a *New York Times* opinion piece titled "Good for Google, Bad for America." Thiel argued that by opening an AI lab in Beijing, Google had to know that it was helping the Chinese military. The Chinese have a "civil-military fusion" principle, which mandates that all research done in China be shared with the People's Liberation Army, Thiel said in 2017.[28]

So Google and its employees have no problems working for the Chinese military but see a lot of ethical issues when working with the US military. Ironically, Google as a company could not have been founded in China. It would have been censored and maybe even have its founders imprisoned.

Tech giants have become so popular and powerful that they are essentially controlling people's lives. Unfortunately, these companies have not shied away from wielding this power. Ironically, the social media industry, which came about because of the belief in freedom of speech, has grown to become censorship boards. In the 2020 election aftermath, anybody who questioned the election was censored.

During the coronavirus pandemic, social media censored what it saw as dangerous and misleading information. Even some leading scientists had their posts taken down simply because what they said was not in line with what the Centers for Disease Control and Prevention (CDC) had put out to the public.

Speaking on CNN, the YouTube CEO, Susan Wojcicki, said that her company removes "information that is problematic, anything that is medically unsubstituted; people saying like, 'Take Vitamin C, take turmeric' . . . those are the examples of things that could be a violation of our policy." In the interview, Wojcicki speaks with so much authority on the coronavirus, you would think she had a PhD in epidemiology, or that YouTube had a panel of PhD epidemiology experts advising it. As Tucker Carlson observed, Wojcicki's background does not qualify her to speak with such authority on this subject.[29]

YouTube, just like other social media companies, largely relies on CDC guidelines, the same CDC that in January 2022 was mocked and criticized for putting out inconsistent incoherent guidelines on COVID. As comedian Jimmy Fallon joked then, "CDC's slogan should just be, 'We have no idea.'" [30]

By censoring the public, Silicon Valley is taking on a task it neither understands properly nor is prepared for. Quite a number of Silicon Valley players, including major founders, dropped out of formal schooling when they realized they had exceptional talent for coding and high tech. Some of them dropped out of high school, others from undergraduate studies. As intelligent as these people are, their expertise is very narrow. They do not have the benefit of formal education, which equips learners with a wide range of knowledge. They are certainly not equipped with enough knowledge to act as fact checkers and censors for the public.

There is no substitute to letting information flow and allowing the public to make their own decisions.

NOTES

1. Newton, Casey. "Everything you need to know about section 230," The Verge, December 29, 2020, 4:50PM EST. https://www.theverge.com/21273768/section-230 -explained-internet-speech-law-definition-guide-free-moderation

2. Ibid.

3. Murdock. Jason. "Twitter under pressure over 'double standards' after Donald Trump, MAGA crackdown," *Newsweek*, January 15, 2021, 11:14 AM EST. https://www.newsweek.com/twitter-donald-trump-maga-crackdown-double-standards -content-moderation-1561918

4. Ibid.

5. Dwoskin, Elizabeth, and Tiku, Nitasha. "How Twitter, on the front lines of history, finally decided to ban Trump," *Washington Post*, January 16, 2021. https://www .washingtonpost.com/technology/2021/01/16/how-twitter-banned-trump/

6. Ibid.

7. Ibid.

8. Browne, Ryan. "Germany's Merkel hits out at Twitter over 'problematic' Trump ban," *Newsweek*, January 11, 2021. https://www.cnbc.com/2021/01/11/germanys -merkel-hits-out-at-twitter-over-problematic-trump-ban.html

9. Ibid.

10. Ibid.

11. Lipn, Michael. "Twitter bans Trump, removes tweet by Iran's Khamenei on same day, sparking 'double standards' backlash," Voice of America, January 9, 2021. https://www.voanews.com/a/silicon-valley-technology_twitter-bans-trump-removes-tweet-irans-khamenei-same-day-sparking-double/6200516.html

12. Ibid.

13. Ibid.

14. Ibid.

15. Ibid.

16. Ibid.

17. Jones, Dustin. "Twitter bans account linked to Iran's supreme leader," NPR, January 22, 2021. https://www.npr.org/2021/01/22/959736537/twitter-bans-account-linked-to-irans-supreme-leader

18. Moore, Mark. "Twitter bans account linked to Iran's supreme leader over Trump assassination threat," *New York Post*, January 16, 2022. https://nypost.com/2022/01/16/twitter-bans-account-linked-to-irans-khamenei-over-trump-assassination-threat/

19. Starr, Michael, and Reich, Aaron. "Account linked to Iran supreme leader banned from Twitter," *Jerusalem Post*, January 16, 2022. https://www.jpost.com/breaking-news/article-692712

20. Palmer, Alex W. "The man behind China's aggressive new voice," *New York Times*, July 7, 2021. https://www.nytimes.com/2021/07/07/magazine/china-diplomacy-twitter-zhao-lijian.html

21. Zhao Lijian. Twitter Post, March 12, 2020, 7:37 AM, PST. https://twitter.com/zlj517/status/1238111898828066823?s=20

22. *Post* Editorial Board. "One year later, The Post's Hunter Biden reporting is vindicated—but still buried," *New York Post*, October 12, 2021. https://nypost.com/2021/10/12/one-year-later-the-posts-hunter-biden-reporting-is-vindicated-but-still-buried/

23. Paul, Kari. "Facebook and Twitter restrict controversial New York Post story on Joe Biden," *The Guardian*, October 14, 2020. https://www.theguardian.com/technology/2020/oct/14/facebook-twitter-new-york-post-hunter-biden

24. Ibid.

25. Paul, Kari. "Presidential taxes: Long-concealed records show Trump's chronic losses and years of tax avoidance," *New York Times*, September 27, 2020. https://www.nytimes.com/interactive/2020/09/27/us/donald-trump-taxes.html

26. Conger, Kate. "Google plans not to renew its contract for Project Maven, a controversial Pentagon drone AI imaging program," Gizmodo, June 1, 2018. https://gizmodo.com/google-plans-not-to-renew-its-contract-for-project-mave-1826488620

27. Ibid.

28. Thiel, Peter. "Good for Google, bad for America," *New York Times*, August 1, 2019. https://www.nytimes.com/2019/08/01/opinion/peter-thiel-google.html

29. Fox News. "Tucker calls out Big Tech over COVID censorship," YouTube, August 12, 2021. https://www.youtube.com/watch?v=skSPOe4Xbf0

30. Flood, Brian. "CDC faces bipartisan scorn after muddled messages leave Americans confused over latest COVID guidelines," Fox News, January 5, 2022. https://www.foxnews.com/media/bipartisan-scorn-for-the-cdc

Chapter 7

Final Word

The fundamental tactics used by the media to control people could be a relic of the Cold War. The propaganda used by the media to achieve its objectives is not unlike Cold War propaganda.

In 2016, just before the presidential elections, a whistleblower platform known as WikiLeaks hacked into John Podesta's email account and stole nearly two hundred thousand pages of emails.[1] John Podesta was the campaign manager for 2016 presidential candidate Hillary Clinton. WikiLeaks was believed to be owned by Julian Assange, the famed whistleblower.

The hacked emails revealed a lot of surprises about the Clinton campaign and the media. None of those surprises, however, was more disturbing than the revelation of just how cozy the Clinton campaign had secretly been with well-known members of the media. While it had always been obvious that the media wanted Clinton to win, it was still shocking to finally discover how corrupt the media was willing to become in order to have Clinton elected.

In one of those emails, John Harwood, the then chief Washington correspondent for CNBC, sought advice from the Clinton campaign as to what questions he should ask a leading Republican candidate at a Republican presidential primary debate hosted by CNBC.

"What should I ask Jeb?"[2] Harwood emailed Clinton's campaign manager on September 21, 2015.

The debate referred to in the email took place on October 28, 2015.[3] Jeb Bush, the former governor of Florida, was one of the participants and was believed, at the time, to be the candidate most likely to face Hillary Clinton in 2016. So, when John Harwood asked the Clinton camp for advice on what question to ask an opposing candidate, he was really crossing the line into journalistic malpractice and corruption.

A telltale sign that they were all doing the same thing was that, after the emails were revealed, members of the mainstream media did not seem to mind at all that one of their colleagues was engaged in such a behavior. There were no calls for him to step down from his position. In fact, he continued in his job as if nothing had happened at all.

In any case, those secret emails should not have been a surprise at all. The media has for a long time been, directly or indirectly, supporting the Democratic Party. This support often comes by the way of selecting which information to report, with the sole intention of influencing their target audience. In other words, the media uses the tactic called "propaganda."

Propaganda has been defined as the selective presentation of information in a manner that is intended to promote a specific train of thought.[4] This tendency by the media to use propaganda to support its chosen candidate is not unlike the tactics the media, under the instructions of the federal government, used in the Cold War when the media was used to keep the American people's support.

Just like the exposed coziness between the media and the Democratic Party in 2016, during the Cold War, the State and Defense Departments were in constant communication with the media bosses to manage and shape public opinion.[5] The tactics used by the media today to support their causes and empower themselves may just be a sign of the proverbial "chicken coming home to roost." The Soviet Union is dead; the Cold War is over. But the press still needs an adversary to propagandize against. And so, it ends up targeting the very citizens it was supposed to serve.

Another reason that sustains the power-hungry media is the fact that the media establishment itself mostly comprises people with little education. Thus, there is very little originality of thought within the media system, and hence a tendency to just parrot whatever the few thought leaders in the industry say. This results in the media having one coordinated message.

The American media likes to look at itself as comprising an educated elite.[6] But that is not true. According to the Career Explorer website, 82 percent of journalists in America hold only a bachelor's degree.[7] While this number is much bigger than the proportion of bachelor's degrees in the general population, a bachelor's degree is not adequate to equip one with skills to analyze the complex world of the twenty-first century.

As the tenth president of the University of Southern California, Steven B. Sample said:

> We have entered an era in which the bachelor's degree for most students is only a prelude to more specialized graduate and post graduate education. The speed at which knowledge is being generated today requires increased specialization. In my own discipline of electrical engineering, it sometimes takes 3 or 4 adjectives to find the precise area of electrical engineering where one inhabits.[8]

To be fair, everywhere in the United States, not just in the media, the power structures are not really based on education. In corporate America, for instance, it is not uncommon to see CEOs or C-Suite executives with minimal educational qualifications. The political elites are not themselves the most educated either, usually holding a BA and/or a law degree, whereas in other countries, leaders—especially political leaders—tend to be highly educated. Take China, for instance.

In the Chinese Communist Party (CCP), education is one of the important factors when choosing leadership. Current Chinese leader, Xi Jinping, has a doctoral degree. In the Chinese Central Committee alone, forty-five members have doctoral degrees.[9] Given that much brain power on their side, perhaps it should not be surprising why the Chinese seem to always be a step ahead of the United States on the international stage. In recent times, China has made headlines with diplomatic initiatives in developing countries and has also achieved big technological successes, including hypersonic weapons, artificial intelligence, and space travel.

Donald Trump used to say that the Chinese "eat our lunch" because, as he put it, "Our leaders are stupid."[10] Incidentally, Joe Biden agreed with him on the idea of the Chinese "eating our lunch."[11] In an interview with David Brooks of the *New York Times*, Biden also said, "We're kind of at a place where the rest of the world is beginning to look to China."[12]

Robert D. Atkinson, president of the Information Technology and Innovation Foundation, also agreed with this assessment. In an article in the *Washington Post*, Atkinson said, "China has been kidney-punching its competitors and has received in return only the occasional sheepish rebuke at ministerial dialogues. Trump is right when he says that China has been eating our lunch and that it is time to do something about it."[13]

It is ironic that Americans often complain that, on the international level, American kids are lagging behind their Chinese counterparts in mathematics and science. In reality though, even the adults—the political, economic, and financial leaders of America—lag behind their Chinese counterparts in education.

The culture of putting less emphasis on education in America enables the media to overrule real experts by bringing people who are not very qualified on a subject to speak with authority as experts. It is a culture that says everybody can do anything, if they just fake it enough. Thus, one consequence of media power is the death of the real expert.

The media appears very uncomfortable talking to real experts on any subject. Perhaps it could be that real experts are expensive; perhaps it is difficult to get real experts to go along with the media's philosophy; perhaps the media does not know who the real experts on a particular subject are.

Take for instance the case of Malaysia Flight MH370, which disappeared without a trace on March 8, 2014. After the shocking news of the disappearance of the flight, as news networks were scrambling to make sense of what was happening, CNN interviewed their own correspondent Richard Quest, whom they called an aviation expert.[14] They also talked to lawyers who had worked with crashes before and to pilots.

Quest is a good reporter. He may well have excellent knowledge of aviation. Pilots too may have very good knowledge of the plane. However, none of these people would have more knowledge about the plane than the expert who designs the plane for a living. Richard Quest has never studied aeronautical or aerospace engineering and could only offer speculations.

So why did the network not bring in an expert plane designer to be the in-house expert at the time?

The same thing is noticed in election coverage. Ideally, reading and analyzing opinion polls requires considerable knowledge of statistics and probability. A look across the media landscape shows that most of the people responsible for this task in the media are themselves not mathematicians or statisticians. They did not learn probability or statistics in school.

It should not be surprising that there are a lot of errors associated with the reading of opinion polls on television. For instance, if a poll has candidate X at 42 percent and candidate Y at 45 percent, and the margin of error is plus or minus 4 percent, it is not uncommon to see the presenter simply claim that candidate Y is winning! If the presenter had been trained in statistics and probability, he would not have said that.

Not everybody can be an expert. Just like Steven B. Sample said, the speed at which knowledge is being generated today requires increased specialization. To be an expert on any subject, especially science, one needs to study up to the PhD level and then engage in research in that particular field for some time. Most of the people who are invited to give opinions on television do not fill the bill.

Bill Nye, popularly known as "Bill Nye the Science Guy," regularly appears on television networks to talk about climate change.[15] According to Wikipedia, Nye has a bachelor's degree in mechanical engineering. He worked at Boeing and is obviously a very smart guy. A bachelor's degree in mechanical engineering, though rigorous, cannot equip him to be an expert on climate change. His conversation with Tucker Carlson on February 27, 2017, was very telling.[16]

Tucker Carlson asked Nye a simple but very scientific question: To what degree is human activity contributing to global warming? Bill Nye could not answer the question.[17] A bachelor's degree in a field does not necessarily mean that one can comment with authority on any specialized area in that field. Even a PhD in a particular field does not mean that the individual has expertise to comment in every area of specialization of that field other than his or her own.

Some of earlier misconceptions surrounding coronavirus knowledge in America were due to the media relying on people who were not exact experts qualified to talk on the coronavirus. For example, not every medical doctor can comment with authority on any emerging disease.

A Doctor of Medicine (MD) is a professional degree. Much like the Doctor of Education (EdD), Doctor of Engineering (DEng), Doctor of Psychology in Clinical Psychology (PsyD), and Juris Doctor (JD), the MD is a degree that focuses on application and analysis of the current state of the art in the field. The award of a professional degree signifies the recipient's deep knowledge in the field as it is today.

On the other hand, a Doctor of Philosophy (PhD) is the university's highest academic degree. It is granted after an advanced course of study, a program of individual research guided by faculty mentors, and preparation and defense of original work of scholarship before a committee of faculty members. PhD students are trained in the fundamental philosophy of a field. They are researchers by training. They are equipped to analyze never seen before phenomena in their fields of specialization.

If there is a flu epidemic in one part of the country, it makes sense to invite an MD—a general practitioner or an emergency room doctor—to give comments or analysis on television. However, when the epidemic involves a never seen before disease such as coronavirus, then a PhD—in this case, a PhD immunologist—is necessary.

In closing the book, it is probably important to look at a few tips that can help media consumers get accurate news, even if the media's intention is to mislead. First, it is important to recognize who the experts are and which one of them is giving an honest analysis. A person can have expertise as discussed above, but then toe a political line when it comes to giving opinions on television or in social media.

Expert analysis is unpredictable. Of course, that is why people pay experts to analyze issues for them. If expert analysis was predictable, there would be no need to pay thousands of dollars. When an expert on television is predictable or says things based on common sense, then that person is either not an expert, is being dishonest, or is just toeing the network line. During the coronavirus pandemic, one expert hired by CNN who appeared frequently on Anderson Cooper's program, always started her answers by "That's right, Anderson."

Anderson Cooper is an expert in broadcasting; he is not a scientist. He cannot always be right on coronavirus. There are many other experts on TV who always answer their question by—to paraphrase—"Democrats are right,

Republicans are wrong," or vice versa. The world cannot always be that predictable.

The second thing to look for in the media is how much the news source is looking at both sides of the issue. There is a new anti-intellectual argument in the media that says that on some issues, there are not two sides because journalists are sure one side is correct. So they do not even bother to look at the other side.

This argument is anti-intellectual, anti-education, and very wrong. Every credible analysis will involve a look at multiple sides of the issue before coming to any conclusion. The old British high school education curriculum used to include "English composition," often given as homework. Usually, students would be asked to write prose on a question by coming up with arguments for and against the topic and then draw a conclusion. Those rules still apply for all credible analysis. Any analyst who simply talks about one side should be looked at with suspicion. There is no such a thing as an extreme left or right analyst because the truth is neither. The analyst's job is to get at the truth.

And for both the media personnel and the media news consumer, educating oneself, formally or otherwise, is crucial in the twenty-first century. Education, not only in one field of study, but also across fields, equips people with knowledge to understand the universe. There is nothing like too much education. As the former USC president put it, the world has become more complex, and it will take disciplined minds to unravel the truth about it.

NOTES

1. Stein, Jeff. "What 20,000 pages of hacked WikiLeaks emails teach us about Hillary Clinton," Vox, October 20, 2016, 9:30 AM EDT. https://www.vox.com/policy-and -politics/2016/10/20/13308108/wikileaks-podesta-hillary-clinton

2. Concha, Joe. "Campaign collusion: Is CNBC's John Harwood too close to the Clinton operation?," *The Hill*, November 7, 2016, 11:05 AM EST. https://thehill.com /blogs/pundits-blog/media/304686-campaign-collusion-is-cnbcs-john-harwood-too -close-to-the-clinton

3. Little, Katie. "Full coverage of GOP presidential debate," CNBC, October 28, 2015, 11:31 PM EDT. https://www.cnbc.com/2015/10/28/gop-presidential-candidates -square-off-in-cnbc-debate.html

4. Mull, Christian, and Matthew Wallin. "Propaganda: A tool of strategic influence." American Security Project, 2013. http://www.jstor.org/stable/resrep06038; Cull, Nicholas J. PowerPoint presentation. "Foreign Service Institute Public Diplomacy 2013."

5. Bernhard, Nancy E. "Clearer than truth: Public affairs television and the State Department's domestic information campaigns, 1947–1952," *Diplomatic History* 21, no. 4 (1997): 545–67. http://www.jstor.org/stable/24913336.

6. Bonn, Tess. "Conservative group: CNN's Don Lemon segment shows what 'elites of America think about the rest of the country,'" *The Hill*, January 29, 2020. https://thehill.com/hilltv/rising/480580-conservative-group-cnns-don-lemon-segment-shows-what-elites-of-america-think-about-the-rest-of-the-country

7. "What education do journalists have?," Career Explorer. https://www.careerexplorer.com/careers/journalist/education/

8. *Ph.D. Hooding Ceremony*, DVD, directed by the Graduate School, University of California (Los Angeles: Take One Productions, 2007).

9. Brar, Aadil. "China's top two leaders have doctoral degrees. In CCP, education also decides political power," The Print, June 23, 2021, 11:34 AM EST. https://theprint.in/opinion/eye-on-china/chinas-top-two-leaders-have-doctoral-degrees-in-ccp-education-also-decides-political-power/682617/

10. Savaransky, Rebecca. "Trump: Our leaders are 'stupid,'" *The Hill*, September 19, 2016. https://thehill.com/blogs/ballot-box/presidential-races/296576-trump-our-leaders-are-stupid;

11. Brunnstrom, David, Alper, Alexandra, and Tain, Yew Lun. "China will 'eat our lunch,' Biden warns after clashing with Xi on most fronts," Reuters, February 10, 2021. https://www.reuters.com/article/us-usa-china/china-will-eat-our-lunch-biden-warns-after-clashing-with-xi-on-most-fronts-idUSKBN2AB06A

12. Brooks, David. "Has Biden changed? He tells us," *New York Times*, May 20, 2021. https://www.nytimes.com/2021/05/20/opinion/joe-biden-david-brooks-interview.html

13. Atkinson, Robert D. "How Trump can stop China from eating our lunch," *Washington Post*, April 5, 2017. https://www.washingtonpost.com/opinions/global-opinions/how-trump-can-stop-china-from-eating-our-lunch/2017/04/05/b83e4460-1953-11e7-bcc2-7d1a0973e7b2_story.html

14. Quest, Richard. "MH370: Did the pilots do it?," CNN, March 8, 2016, 2:38 PM EST. https://www.cnn.com/2016/03/07/asia/mh370-quest-pilots/

15. "Bill Nye," https://en.wikipedia.org/wiki/Bill_Nye

16. "Tucker vs. Bill Nye the Science Guy," YouTube, February 27, 2017. https://www.youtube.com/watch?v=qN5L2q6hfWo

17. Ibid.

Index

About the Author

Cedrick Ngalande is an aerospace engineer and space scientist currently residing in Southern California. He has written op-eds and political analysis pieces for Malawi and South Africa and has also published numerous peer-reviewed scientific papers. He has a PhD in astronautical engineering, a master's in aerospace engineering, a master's in financial engineering, an MBA from the University of Southern California, and a diploma in mechanical engineering from the University of Malawi. He completed his postdoctoral scholarship at the U.S. Naval Research Laboratories in Washington, DC.

Cedrick was born in Malawi in southeastern Africa at a time when Malawi was still a dictatorship. The parallels between the role of the media in Malawi in those dictatorship days and the behavior of the media in America today are very alarming. Cedrick wrote this book as a warning that freedom cannot be taken for granted. While most Americans only know freedom, Cedrick has experienced both tyranny and freedom, and he knows the difference—freedom is much better.

In this book, educators, parents, and students can learn about the dangers of a powerful homogenous press that does not tolerate diversity of thought. Cedrick believes that the school system is the first line of defense for patriotism and democracy. Teachers, from preschool to graduate school, can help to fight this media dictatorship by cultivating independence of thought among students. School administrators, too, have a responsibility to ensure that school campuses are sanctuaries for freedom of thought where leaders of tomorrow are taught to be tolerant of opposing views.

Cedrick's life experience and his expertise in multiple disciplines, from science to business to engineering to finance, give him a unique perspective of the way the media shapes, controls, and sometimes suppresses expert opinion in different fields in order to exercise control over the populace.

www.ingramcontent.com/pod-product-compliance
Lightning Source LLC
Chambersburg PA
CBHW030653270326
41929CB00007B/346